THE LAW OF VIOLENCE AGAINST WOMEN

by
Margaret C. Jasper, Esq.

Oceana's Legal Almanac Series:
Law for the Layperson

1998
Oceana Publications Inc.
Dobbs Ferry, N.Y.

Information contained in this work has been obtained by Oceana Publications from sources believed to be reliable. However, neither the Publisher nor its authors guarantee the accuracy or completeness of any information published herein, and neither Oceana nor its authors shall be responsible for any errors, omissions or damages arising from the use of this information. This work is published with the understanding that Oceana and its authors are supplying information, but are not attempting to render legal or other professional services. If such services are required, the assistance of an appropriate professional should be sought.

You may order this or any other Oceana publications by visiting Oceana's Web Site at http://www.oceanalaw.com

ISBN: 0-379-11325-2 (alk. paper)

Oceana's Legal Almanac Series: Law for the Layperson
ISSN: 1075-7376

Manufactured in the United States of America on acid-free paper.

To My Husband Chris

Your love and support
are my motivation and inspiration

-and-

In memory of my son, Jimmy

ABOUT THE AUTHOR

Margaret C. Jasper is an attorney engaged in the general practice of law in South Salem, New York, concentrating in the areas of personal injury and entertainment law. Ms. Jasper holds a Juris Doctor degree from Pace University School of Law, White Plains, New York, is a member of the New York and Connecticut bars, and is certified to practice before the United States District Courts for the Southern and Eastern Districts of New York, and the United States Supreme Court.

Ms. Jasper has been appointed to the panel of arbitrators of the American Arbitration Association and the law guardian panel for the Family Court of the State of New York, is a member of the Association of Trial Lawyers of America, and is a New York State licensed real estate broker and member of the Westchester County Board of Realtors, operating as Jasper Real Estate, in South Salem, New York.

Ms. Jasper is the author and general editor of the following legal almanacs: Juvenile Justice and Children's Law; Marriage and Divorce; Estate Planning; The Law of Contracts; The Law of Dispute Resolution; Law for the Small Business Owner; The Law of Personal Injury; Real Estate Law for the Homeowner and Broker; Everyday Legal Forms; Dictionary of Selected Legal Terms; The Law of Medical Malpractice; The Law of Product Liability; The Law of No-Fault Insurance; The Law of Immigration; The Law of Libel and Slander; The Law of Buying and Selling; Elder Law; The Right to Die; AIDS Law; The Law of Obscenity and Pornography; The Law of Child Custody; The Law of Debt Collection; Consumer Rights Law; Bankruptcy Law for the Individual Debtor; Victim's Rights Law; Animal Rights Law; Workers' Compensation Law; Employee Rights in the Workplace; Probate Law; Environmental Law; Labor Law; The Americans with Disabilities Act; The Law of Capital Punishment; and Education Law.

TABLE OF CONTENTS

INTRODUCTION

This almanac addresses a serious problem facing American society: violence against women. Violence against women takes many forms, including domestic violence, rape and other sexual assaults. Violent acts against women may be committed by strangers as well as friends, family members and those with whom the victim has had an intimate relationship.

Recognizing the extent of this problem, Congress has taken strong measures to prevent and reduce the incidence of violence against women by enacting The Violence Against Women Act of 1994, an important piece of bipartisan legislation included as part of the Violent Crime Control and Law Enforcement Act of 1994.

Federal action in this area comes at a critical time. According to a recently released Department of Justice Bureau of Justice Statistics report, women are the victims of more than 4.5 million violent crimes each year. Violence against women in America is a national crisis and nobody can afford to look the other way. Statistics demonstrate that violence against women does not discriminate based on race, ethnicity, age, education, income, marital status or residence.

This almanac examines the many aspects of violence against women, and the legislative efforts to address these crimes. The various provisions of The Violence Against Women Act are set forth, and their impact on domestic violence and sexual assault. In addition, legislative enactments designed to address the problems facing immigrant women and children who are victims of domestic violence are also discussed.

The Appendices provide resource directories, applicable statutes, and other pertinent information and data. The Glossary contains definitions of many of the terms used throughout the almanac.

CHAPTER 1:

AN OVERVIEW

In General

According to the U.S. Department of Justice Bureau of Justice Statistics ("BJS"), women are the victims of more than 4.5 million violent crimes each year. This alarming figure includes approximately 500,000 rapes or other sexual assaults.

Estimating rates of violence against women, especially sexual assaults and other offenses committed by intimates, continues to be a difficult task because many women choose not to report these crimes to law enforcement authorities. There is a general belief that no purpose would be served by reporting these crimes. Sexual attacks, in particular, are perceived as too personal to reveal, and many women feel that the subsequent investigation subjects them to additional trauma.

In an effort to improve their data on crimes committed against women which are particularly difficult to track, such as rape, sexual assault and domestic violence, the BJS redesigned its National Crime Victimization Survey. Approximately 50,000 households and more than 100,000 individuals participate in this nationwide survey annually. The redesigned survey format gives additional information on rapes, sexual assaults and domestic violence that was not previously available. The BJS survey attempts to measure crime from the victim's perspective.

The Violence Against Women Act of 1994

The Violence Against Women Act ("VAWA") was enacted as part of the Violent Crime Control and Law Enforcement Act of 1994 (the "Crime Bill"). The VAWA is landmark bipartisan legislation which sets forth firm law enforcement tactics and includes important safeguards for female victims of domestic violence and sexual assault. In its first year, the VAWA and its related provisions proved extremely effective in preventing domestic violence and providing protection for women against violent sex offenders.

Following is an outline of the most important aspects of the VAWA, many of which are discussed more fully elsewhere in this almanac:

Subtitle A: Safe Streets for Women

Subtitle A of the VAWA is entitled "The Safe Streets for Women Act of 1994" (Subtitle A: Section 40101 et seq.) and includes the following important safeguards for female victims of violence:

1. Chapter 1 provides for stiffer federal penalties for repeat sex crime offenders; authorizes mandatory restitution enforceable by victims of sex crimes; and provides funding to the U.S. Attorney's Office for the purpose of hiring federal victim/witness counselors in connection with the prosecution of sex and domestic violence crimes.

2. Chapter 2 provides funding designed to reduce the incidence of violent crime against women by assisting the States, Indian tribal governments, and local governments with monetary grants to train law enforcement officers and prosecutors to more effectively respond to such crimes, and to develop and strengthen victim services programs. Grant eligibility requires that participating entities carry the cost of medical examinations for victims of sexual assault, and do not assess any costs against the victim in connection with the filing of criminal charges.

3. Chapter 3 provides monetary grants for the purposes of making capital improvements—e.g. lighting, camera surveillance and security telephone systems—to prevent crime in public transportation systems and parks.

4. Chapter 4 makes an important amendment to the Federal Rules of Evidence, limiting inquiries into a victim's past sexual behavior or predisposition.

5. Chapter 5 provides monetary grants to operate rape prevention/education programs and hotlines; prepare informational materials to increase public awareness about sexual assault; and to effectively train professionals, such as probation and parole officers, who work with released sex offenders, in their treatment and supervision. Chapter 5 also provides for confidentiality of communications between victims and their counselors.

The full text of Subtitle A is set forth in Appendix 1.

Subtitle B: Safe Homes for Women

Subtitle B of the VAWA is entitled "The Safe Homes for Women Act of 1994" (Subtitle B: Section 40201 et seq.) and includes the following important safeguards for female victims of violence:

1. Chapter 1 provides funding for a National Domestic Violence Hotline;

2. Chapter 2 provides for interstate enforcement of domestic violence offenses, making it a crime to cross state lines to continue to abuse a spouse or partner; and authorizes mandatory restitution enforceable by victims of domestic violence. Chapter 2 also provides that protection orders are entitled to full faith and credit by the courts of another state or Indian tribe with the same enforceability as if that state or Indian tribe had issued the order.

3. Chapter 3 provides monetary grants to encourage States, Indian tribal governments and local governments to treat domestic violence as a serious criminal offense, and to implement mandatory arrest programs for domestic violence crimes and protection order violations.

4. Chapter 4 provides monetary grants for the purpose of funding and operating battered women's shelters.

5. Chapter 5 implements programs designed to educate young people about domestic violence on age appropriate levels.

6. Chapter 6 provides for monetary grants to nonprofit private organizations for the purposes of establishing prevention/intervention domestic violence projects in local communities.

7. Chapter 8 provides for confidentiality of domestic violence shelters and the addresses of abuse victims.

8. Chapter 9 authorizes research contracts for the purpose of studying violence against women, including sexual assault and domestic violence. A panel of the National Academy of Sciences is developing a research agenda to increase the understanding and control of violence against women, including rape and domestic violence. In addition, research evaluation of programs addressing violence against women will provide important information on their implementation and effectiveness in order to refine and improve the programs.

9. Chapter 10 provides monetary grants to States, Indian tribal governments and local governments of rural States, and to other public or private entities of rural States, for the education, prevention, investigation and prosecution of domestic violence and child abuse, and to implement treatment and counseling services to such victims.

The full text of the Subtitle B is set forth in Appendix 2.

Subtitle C: Civil Rights for Women

Subtitle C of the VAWA is entitled the "Civil Rights Remedies for Gender-Motivated Violence Act" (Subtitle C: Section 40301 et seq.). The stated purpose of this section is to protect the civil rights of victims of gender motivated violence, and to promote public safety, health, and activities affecting interstate commerce by establishing a Federal civil rights cause of action for victims of crimes of violence motivated by gender. This section also authorizes attorney's fees for the victim. This civil rights remedy was designed to complement existing federal civil rights laws which do not protect women from gender-motivated violence. Now, for the first time, victims of gender-motivated violent crimes, such as rape and domestic violence, have the right to sue their attackers for damages under federal law.

The full text of Subtitle C is set forth in Appendix 3.

Subtitle D: Equal Justice for Women in the Courts

Subtitle D of the VAWA is entitled the "Equal Justice for Women in the Courts Act of 1994" (Subtitle D: Section 40401 et seq.). This section provides monetary grants for the purpose of developing programs for training judges and court personnel in the states, and training tribal judges and court personnel in Indian tribal governments, about sexual assault, domestic violence and other crimes of violence motivated by gender.

The full text of Subtitle D is set forth in Appendix 4.

Subtitle E: Violence Against Women Act Improvements

Subtitle E of the VAWA strengthens the provisions of the Act by providing for pre-trial detention in sex offense cases; increasing penalties against victims below the age of 16; requiring payment for the cost of testing victims for sexually transmitted diseases in sex offense cases; requiring defendants in sex offense cases to be tested for HIV/AIDS disease; strengthening the restitution provisions by enforcing restitution orders through suspension of the defendants' federal benefits; and providing for studies on campus sexual assault and battered women's syndrome.

The full text of Subtitle E is set forth in Appendix 5.

Subtitle F: National Stalker and Domestic Violence Reduction

Subtitle F of the VAWA is entitled "National Stalker and Domestic Violence Reduction" (Subtitle F: Section 40601 et seq.). This section authorizes access to federal criminal information databases for use in domestic violence or stalking cases; and provides monetary grants to States and local governmental units to improve methods of entering data regarding stalking and domestic violence incidents into local, State and national crime information databases.

The full text of Subtitle F is set forth in Appendix 6.

Subtitle G: Protections for Battered Immigrant Women and Children

Subtitle G of the VAWA is entitled "Protections for Battered Immigrant Women and Children" (Subtitle G: Section 40701 et seq.). This section provides that an alien who is the spouse of a U.S. Citizen or legal permanent resident, residing in the United States, who has been battered by or has been the subject of extreme cruelty perpetrated by the spouse, may avoid deportation and/or petition for classification, along with the alien's children.

The full text of Subtitle G is set forth in Appendix 7.

Program Administration under the VAWA

Most VAWA programs are administered either by the U.S. Department of Justice ("DOJ") or the Department of Health and Human Services ("HHS").

The DOJ has taken an aggressive position in fighting violence against women, and works closely with state, tribal authorities, local law enforcement, and other federal agencies in this endeavor. The DOJ administers monetary grant programs to states to help strengthen law enforcement and prosecution of domestic violence, and to improve victim services in these cases.

The DOJ's Community Oriented Policing Services ("COPS") Office has also implemented a program—The Community Policing to Combat Domestic Violence Program—to apply community policing strategies to fight domestic violence. Collaboration is the focus of this initiative which is open to police departments and sheriffs offices that are interested in applying community policing techniques to fight domestic violence. The DOJ will also be releasing guidelines to help states create effective registration systems for people convicted of sexually violent crimes.

HHS is also responsible for administering domestic violence programs in addition to the VAWA, including the Family Violence Prevention and Services Act, which supports battered women's shelters, information and referral services, and public education prevention campaigns.

In addition, the Center for Disease Control ("CDC") has been given a new initiative to research the prevalence of domestic violence.

The S.T.O.P Violence Against Women Grant Program

Over a 5-year period, a total of $800 million in federal funds was authorized under the VAWA to assist states in restructuring law enforcement's response to violent crimes against women. All 50 states and eligible territories received designated funds under the Office of Justice Programs "S.T.O.P. ("Services/Training/Officers/Prosecutors") Violence Against Women Grant Program." The formula grants to states are allocated according to population, with each state guaranteed a base amount.

The S.T.O.P grant program requires states to develop a joint strategy to combat violence against women. The program requires and encourages collaboration among victim advocates, prosecutors, and law enforcement authorities.

As a condition to receiving grants, states must certify that they will incur full out-of-pocket costs of forensic medical examinations for victims of sexual assault. They must also certify that within two years, victims of sexual assault will bear no costs associated with the filing of criminal charges or protection orders.

Because of the condition for receiving grants, several states have passed laws or changed their administrative procedures to fund all forensic medical examinations for victims of sexual assault, thereby ensuring that criminal investigations in sexual assault cases are funded like all other criminal investigations—by the state and not by the victim.

The Department also has awarded approximately $1 million to tribal governments through its "S.T.O.P. Violence Against Indian Women Discretionary Grant Program," with the goal of strengthening the response of tribal court systems to violent crimes against women.

Studies

A number of studies authorized under the Act are being finalized—including evaluation of needed improvements in incidence reporting, a report on the problem of sexual assault on college campuses, a study of the use of battered women's syndrome evidence at trial, and an assessment of ways to protect the confidentiality of address information for victims of domestic violence.

Once completed, all of these VAWA studies will provide a more complete and accurate picture of the nature and extent of violence against women and improve the ability to track and respond to these crimes.

Department of Justice Violence Against Women Office

The DOJ's Violence Against Women Office is headed by Bonnie J. Campbell, who was appointed to this position by President Clinton. Ms. Campbell is responsible for the overall coordination and focus of Department of Justice efforts to combat violence against women, serving as the primary point of contact for other federal agencies, state and local governments, outside organizations, and Congress.

Within the DOJ, Ms. Campbell works closely with the COPS Director, Joseph Brann, and with community police officers to help reduce domestic violence and other crimes against women in America's neighborhoods. She also works extensively with the DOJ's Office of Justice Programs Bureaus, the Offices of Policy Development and Legislative Affairs, the FBI and the Criminal Divisions, and the 93 U.S. Attorneys.

The Violence Against Women Office is also spearheading an employee awareness campaign to educate DOJ employees on domestic violence issues. The campaign includes a training video, information fair, workplace guidelines and educational materials.

This DOJ program will serve as a model for other federal agencies which were also directed by President Clinton to initiate workplace awareness efforts on domestic violence. A Violence Against Women Office internet home page is also designed to provide access to the latest information on efforts relating to domestic violence and sexual assault, as well as links to other sources of information on these subjects.

The Violence Against Women Office and the Advisory Council, discussed further below, work together to promote greater awareness of the problem of violence against women, and to find effective solutions.

Advisory Council on Violence Against Women

In July 1995, a joint Advisory Council on Violence Against Women was formed under the auspices of the Department of Justice and the Department of Health and Human Services to help coordinate efforts to fight violence against women across America.

This group of national leaders from a variety of fields and professions was put together in order to provide Attorney General Janet Reno and the Secretary of Health and Human Services Donna Shalala with practical and general policy advice concerning implementation of the VAWA.

The Advisory Council's 46 members draw on the many different professions that can help fight violence against women and assist victims. The council members include leaders in public health, victims rights, social services, the business community, higher education, law enforcement, religious groups, and other fields. Members were selected based on their experience and commitment to fighting violence against women, particularly domestic violence and sexual assault.

The Advisory Council's stated mission is to promote greater awareness of the problem of violence against women and its victims, to help devise solutions, and to advise the federal government as it implements the VAWA.

As opinion leaders in their respective communities, Advisory Council members play a vital role in changing societal perceptions and in spreading the message that violence against women is unacceptable and detrimental to our entire society. Members will also promote coordination between law enforcement and health care agencies, between the public and private sectors, and among federal, state and local governments, to create a seamless system that addresses the diverse needs of women and families in crisis.

Some of the members well known for their work in the area of violence against women include:

1. Gail Abarbanel, Director, Rape Treatment Center of Santa Monica Hospital Medical Center. In 1974, Ms. Abarbanel founded the Rape Treatment Center which provides free services to sexual assault victims and their families. She has continually worked as a national educator on sexual assault by speaking to law enforcement, medical professionals, and the media. In 1991, she was honored by the President for her work helping victims and raising awareness about sexual assault.

2. Michael P. Barnes, President, National District Attorneys' Association; Prosecuting Attorney for St. Joseph County, Indiana. Mr. Barnes has been prosecuting cases in St. Joseph County for over 20 years, and has been repeatedly recognized for his work with victims of crime. In 1989, he received an award for Outstanding Service to Victims from the Domestic Violence Coalition of Indiana and was given the Victims of Crime Award from the Department of Justice Law Enforcement Coordinating Committee in 1992.

3. Larry A. Bedard, M.D., Chairman, Advisory Committee for the American Medical Association Campaign Against Family Violence.

4. Carl C. Bell, M.D., Clinical Professor of Psychiatry, University of Illinois School of Medicine.

5. Alana Bowman, Supervising Deputy, Domestic Violence Prosecution Unit of the Office of the Los Angeles City Attorney. Ms. Bowman has worked on battered women's issues since 1971, when she co-founded a women's legal clinic while at the Washington University School of Law. She is currently chair of the Los Angeles County Domestic Violence Council and sits on the board of the California State Alliance

Against Domestic Violence, the California League of Women Prosecutors and the Southern California Coalition for Battered Women.

6. Reginald K. Brack, Jr., Chairman, Time, Inc. He also serves as chair of the Board of Trustees of the National Urban League and the director of the Advertising Educational Foundation.

7. Sarah M. Buel, Assistant District Attorney, Norfolk County District Attorney's Office. Since graduating from Harvard Law School in 1990, Ms. Buel has worked in District Attorney's Offices across Massachusetts prosecuting domestic violence cases. She has taught seminars on domestic violence for both medical and law school students as well as law enforcement personnel.

8. Lem Burnham, PhD, Director of NFL Player Programs, National Football League. Mr. Burnham leads the player programs of 28 NFL clubs including the Family Assistance Program which includes a national referral network of over 125 professionals.

9. Hon. Karen Burstein, Former New York State Family Court Judge. Ms. Burstein has served New York in several capacities including Auditor General, State Senator, Family Court Judge, and participant in numerous commissions which have furthered the rights of minorities, workers, and women. She currently co-chairs the Advisory Committee of the Office for the Prevention of Domestic Violence, which she was instrumental in creating.

10. Hon. Jane Campbell (D-OH), President, National Council of State Legislators (NCSL). Rep. Campbell has devoted herself to family health and safety issues, serving in the National Conference of States Legislators on the Children and Families Committee and the Welfare Reform Task Force, and in the State Legislature chairing the Abused, Neglected and Dependent Children Oversight Committee. She has used her position to pass legislation beneficial to women and families including insuring the distribution of funds to Domestic Violence Shelters.

CHAPTER 2:

VIOLENCE BETWEEN INTIMATES

In General

Violence between intimates refers to violent acts which are perpetrated by someone with whom the victim has had an intimate relationship. An "intimate" generally refers to one's spouse or ex-spouse, boyfriend or girlfriend. An intimate would not include strangers, friends, or other relatives, such as siblings, parents, in-laws, etc. The violent acts include murder, rape, robbery and assault.

The rate of violence between intimates is difficult to accurately track because many victims do not report these incidents. According to the National Crime Victimization Survey ("NCVS"), the reasons female victims are reluctant to report violent crimes perpetrated by intimates is that they believe the incidents are too personal, or that they fear retaliation from the offender.

Nevertheless, the Department of Justice Bureau of Justice Statistics ("BJS") has used a number of sources to try and determine the prevalence of violence between intimates, including:

1. Statistics from the NCVS which produces estimates of violence based on the perceptions of victims willing to report to interviewers. The NCVS survey includes victims' perceptions on such violent crimes as rape, robbery and assault. Murder is not included due to the obvious unavailability of the victims.

2. Murder statistics are gathered from both the FBI Supplemental Homicide Report from the Uniform Crime Reports program, and BJS studies of murder cases from law enforcement files in large urban counties.

3. The Law Enforcement Management and Administrative Statistics survey provides information on police policies and domestic violence.

4. Surveys of inmates in local jails and state correctional facilities provides information about confined violent offenders.

According to BJS studies, intimates commit an annual average of 621,015 rapes, robberies or assaults, which represents 13% of all such violent offenses. About 15% of the murders committed in 1992 involved intimate offenders.

While friends and acquaintances of women victims committed more than half of the rapes and sexual assaults, intimates committed 26 percent, and strangers were responsible for about one in five.

According to the BJS, in 1992, approximately 28 percent of female homicide victims—approximately 1,414—were known to have been killed by their husbands, former husbands or boyfriends. In contrast, just over 3 percent of male homicide victims—approximately 637—were known to have been killed by their wives, former wives or girlfriends.

In fact, women were attacked about six times more often by offenders with whom they had an intimate relationship than were male violence victims during 1992 and 1993. Men, however, were more likely than women to experience violent crimes committed by both acquaintances and strangers. In fact, men were about twice as likely as women to experience acts of violence by strangers.

A Table representing the trends in the number and rates of homicide victims by relationship to the offender from 1977 through 1992 is set forth in Appendix 8.

Weapon Use

Approximately 18% of rape, robbery and assault victims faced an intimate who was armed compared to those attacked by strangers (33%) other relatives (22%) and acquaintances (21%). In 40% of the intimate victimizations, a knife or sharp instrument was the weapon of choice, guns were involved in 34% of the attacks, and 15% of the attacks involved other weapons. Guns were more likely to be used in attacks by strangers. Nevertheless, women were actually injured by intimates in 52 percent of the attacks, compared to 20 percent of the attacks by strangers.

Approximately 62% of murder victims killed by intimates in 1992 were shot to death. Guns were used to kill wives or ex-wives 69% of the time, and girlfriends in 60% of those cases. Husbands and ex-husbands were also primarily killed by guns in 61% of the homicides, whereas knives were used to murder boyfriends 54% of the time.

Nevertheless, murders involving guns was less for victims killed by intimates than for victims killed by strangers or acquaintances.

Profile of the Victim

Women between the ages of 20 and 34 were the most likely of all ages to be victimized by an intimate. In addition, women of all races were about equally vulnerable to attacks by intimates. Nevertheless, women in families with incomes below $10,000 per year were more likely than other women to be violently attacked by an intimate.

Women living in central cities, suburban areas and rural locations experience similar rates of violence committed by intimates. Divorced or separated women had higher rates of violence by intimates than married women or women who never married. College graduates had the lower rates of violence committed by intimates compared to women with less than a high school education.

Profile of the Offender

Over half of the defendants convicted of killing their spouse had prior criminal records, although they were less likely to have a criminal history than defendants who had killed nonfamily members. In addition, as compared to nonfamily murder defendants, intimates were less likely to be unemployed, but more likely to have a history of mental illness.

Statistics gathered from a 1988 study of murder cases in large urban counties determined that the majority of defendants who killed their spouses were male (60%) and over the age of 30 (77%), as compared to the majority of defendants who killed nonfamily murders, who were overwhelmingly male (93%) and under the age of 30 (65%).

Approximately 80% of the defendants in the 1988 study of spousal murder cases were convicted or pleaded guilty.

Profile of a Spousal Murder Case

According to the BJS, over one third of spousal murders took place during the day, the majority of which took place at home (86%). Most defendants murdered only their spouse. Over half of the defendants had been drinking alcohol at the time of the murder, and almost half of the victims had also been drinking at the time the offense took place.

In approximately 23% of the incidents, the murdered spouses allegedly precipitated the incident by provoking the defendant, e.g. with a deadly weapon, nonlethal weapon or other physical contact.

In addition, over 62% of the defendants accused of murdering their spouses were arrested on the day the crime took place as compared to 32% of defendants accused of killing nonfamily members.

Penalties for Male versus Female Defendants

According to the BJS statistics for spousal murder cases in large urban counties in 1988, women defendants were more likely to be acquitted, or to have their case diverted, rejected or dismissed. Of men convicted of killing their wives, 94% were sentenced to prison, including 15% who were sentenced to life terms. However, women who killed their husbands were less likely to receive a prison sentence—81% were sentenced to prison including 8% who received life terms. In addition, the average prison sentence for women convicted of killing their husbands was 6.2 years as compared to men convicted of killing their wives, who received an average of 17.5 years.

Further, according to a 1991 BJS Survey of inmates in state correctional facilities, female prisoners are more likely than male prisoners to have harmed an intimate—25% of female prisoners versus 10% of male prisoners had harmed an intimate. In addition, approximately one-third of female prisoners incarcerated for homicide had killed their husband, ex-husband or boyfriend.

CHAPTER 3:

DOMESTIC VIOLENCE

In General

Domestic violence generally refers to felony or misdemeanor crimes of violence committed by a current or former spouse of the victim, by a person with whom the victim shares a child in common, by a person who is cohabitating or has cohabitated with the victim as a spouse, or by a person similarly situated to a spouse. Historically, domestic violence was often viewed as a private family matter, and that it was nobody's right to interfere.

Law enforcement often took the position that domestic violence was not a criminal offense. The victim was all too often blamed for causing the abusive behavior—e.g. "button pushing." As a result, the victim frequently remained silent about the abuse, rather than suffer criticism and shame, and possible retaliation by the abuser for involving the police.

By enacting the Violence Against Women Act of 1994 ("VAWA"), the federal government has demonstrated its commitment, along with States, local governmental units, and tribal governments, to put an end to the silence, to create tougher legislation, and to require greater police protection for domestic violence victims. As further discussed below, Subtitle B of the Act—The Safe Homes for Women Act—addresses many important domestic violence concerns.

Protection Orders

A domestic violence victim is often advised to obtain a protection order. A protection order is basically an injunction issued by the court for the purpose of preventing violent or threatening acts of domestic violence. A protection order in à domestic relationship is usually obtained by filing a petition with the Family Court of the jurisdiction where the victim lives. An order of protection is issued on either a temporary or permanent basis.

The court will likely issue a temporary order of protection, upon the filing of the petition, based on the victim's allegations that she is in imminent danger of physical harm. The abuser is entitled to respond to the allegations contained in the petition for a protection order. If it is determined that the allegations are true, a permanent protection order will be issued. The maximum length of time a protection order may last varies according to state law.

A typical protection order may (i) prohibit the abuser from contacting the victim; (ii) prohibit the abuser from further abusing or harassing the victim;

(iii) require the abuser to provide support to the victim and children; and/or (iv) require the abuser to seek counseling.

After a victim has obtained a protection order, she can call the police if the abuser violates it. In some states, police are required to arrest the abuser if there appears to be a violation, e.g. the abuser is found outside the victim's home. Unfortunately, statistics have shown that no piece of paper can completely protect a domestic violence victim from an abuser who is intent on causing physical harm.

Full Faith and Credit Provision

The VAWA's "full faith and credit" provision requires states to honor protection orders issued by other jurisdictions. The U.S. Department of Justice ("DOJ") is devising an aggressive strategy for implementation of this protection for battered women who hold protection orders and move to another state, only to have their abusers follow them there. The following case history demonstrates the importance of giving full faith and credit to out-of-state protection orders, and the need for public awareness of this important VAWA provision.

In February 1993, a woman living in Metropolis, Illinois went to court to obtain a protection order against her abusive live-in boyfriend. The police escorted the woman home and searched the house to make sure her boyfriend was not on the premises. Unknown to police, the boyfriend was hiding in the house.

After the police left, the boyfriend left his hiding place in the ceiling of the woman's home and threatened her. The police were summoned, however, the boyfriend was not arrested because the police had not witnessed the protection order violation. A few months later, the woman was severely beaten by her boyfriend.

Officials at the Metropolis Domestic Violence Center immediately and covertly relocated the woman to Paducah, Kentucky, a larger town just across the Ohio River from Metropolis. Shortly thereafter, the woman was again beaten and her Paducah apartment was destroyed by arson. The woman's boyfriend was convicted and sent to jail for the beating.

After spending a few months in jail, the boyfriend was released. He followed the woman to a Paducah gas station. He kidnapped, beat and sexually assaulted her. When the woman was found in Kentucky, local police declined to arrest the boyfriend because they deemed the Illinois protection order to be invalid within the Kentucky borders. This man was never arrested for the assault, and the victim was told her only relief would be to seek an emergency protection order in a Kentucky court.

When the Metropolis Domestic Violence Center questioned the Paducah Police as to why the woman's Illinois protection order had not been upheld under the Full Faith and Credit provision of the Violence Against Women Act, they responded that they had never heard of such a provision. As a result, the Illinois Attorney General issued a two page fact sheet describing the major provisions of the Violence Against Women Act, including the Full Faith and Credit provision. This information sheet has since been posted on the bulletin boards of local police stations.

The VAWA provides that a civil protection order issued by the court of one State or Indian Tribe (the "issuing state or tribe") shall be accorded full faith and credit by the court of another State or Indian Tribe (the "enforcing state or tribe"), and shall be enforced as if it were the order of the court of the second state or tribe.

Nevertheless, failure by the issuing state to satisfy due process requirements will not entitle a protection order to full faith and credit. The issuing court must have had both personal and subject matter jurisdiction and the respondent must have received reasonable notice and an opportunity to be heard for the provision to be in effect.

In addition, mutual protection orders are not entitled to full faith and credit if a cross or counter petition, complaint or other written pleading has not been filed seeking such a protection order, or if a cross or counter petition has been filed and the order was issued upon a showing of mutual abuse.

Prior to the enactment of the VAWA, a victim with a protection order often could not use that order as the basis for protection if the victim went to work, traveled or moved to another state. Under the "full faith and credit" provision, the second state must enforce the order issued by another jurisdiction, even if the victim otherwise would be ineligible for protection in the second state. A victim does not have to wait for abuse to occur in the second state nor does a victim need to be concerned if he or she cannot meet its jurisdictional requirements.

Furthermore, a victim does not have to register a protection order in the second state for it to be effective. The protection order of the issuing state provides continuous protection to the victim.

The DOJ has made the implementation of the VAWA "full faith and credit" provision a top priority, and has adopted an aggressive multi-faceted implementation campaign involving federal leadership through outreach, research and the provision of training, technical assistance and opportunities for collaboration at the national and state or district levels.

In addition, the National Crime Information Center Protection Order File, which all states should be linked to by 1998, is designed to provide information on protection orders for use in domestic abuse cases. This data will also interface with the National Instant Criminal Background Check System in order to identify those persons prohibited from purchasing a firearm, as further discussed below.

Federal Interstate Domestic Violence Enforcement

Victims of domestic violence often seek safety and shelter with friends and relatives living in other states, where they are often followed by their abusers. The VAWA addressed this problem by establishing new federal offenses in cases where an abuser crosses state lines to violate a protection order or injure, harass or intimidate a spouse or intimate partner.

These provisions are crucial to prosecuting cases where the abuser's travel across state lines makes state prosecution difficult, and/or where state penalties may not be tough enough to deter the abusive behavior. They also provide additional important benefits for domestic violence victims, including strengthened restitution provisions and the right to address the court prior to a pre-trial release of the defendant regarding the victim's concerns about danger posed by the defendant's release.

The VAWA authorizes severe federal sentences for abusers who travel interstate with the intent to injure, harass or intimidate a domestic partner or violate a protection order. The VAWA ensures that the law follows an abuser who crosses state lines, and provides victims with protection throughout the United States.

As set forth below, the DOJ's first successful conviction under the VAWA's interstate domestic violence enforcement provision occurred in the Southern District of West Virginia.

In November 1994, Christopher Bailey of St. Albans, West Virginia beat his wife Sonya until she collapsed. He then placed her in the trunk of their car and drove for five days through West Virginia and Kentucky before taking her to a hospital emergency room. Sonya Bailey suffered irreversible brain damage and remains in a permanent vegetative state.

Under the VAWA's prohibition against interstate domestic violence, federal prosecutors in West Virginia were able to secure a conviction against Christopher Bailey, who was sentenced to life in prison for the kidnapping and interstate domestic violence perpetrated against his wife.

This case illustrates the value of federal action against interstate domestic violence. Although Mr. Bailey was arrested in Kentucky, local police dropped the charges because they were unable to document what had occurred in their jurisdiction. Under West Virginia law, Mr. Bailey might have received less than a two-year sentence for his brutal assault. In contrast, under the federal law, Mr. Bailey received a life sentence.

As set forth below, the nation's second conviction under the VAWA's interstate domestic violence prohibition occurred in the Eastern District of California.

Ricky Steele abused and beat his domestic partner in Oregon, and then forced her to drive with him to California. Mr. Steele was subsequently arrested, convicted under federal law, required to make restitution to his victim, and sentenced to 87 months in prison.

Federal prosecutors have initiated other cases under the VAWA interstate domestic violence prohibition against traveling across state lines with the intent of violating court issued protection orders.

Wayne Hayes was indicted in the Eastern District of New York on charges of traveling interstate with the intention of violating a court order that prohibited him from harassing his ex-wife, and mailing threatening communications to her.

This indictment marks the first use of the VAWA provision that prohibits traveling across a state line in order to violate certain protection orders. The DOJ continues to work with state and local law enforcement to combat interstate domestic violence and identify those cases where use of these new federal remedies is appropriate.

Firearms Disability Provision

The Violent Crime Control and Law Enforcement Act of 1994 (the "Crime Bill") includes a provision that makes it unlawful for persons subject to certain restraining orders to possess firearms. This provision is designed to protect victims of domestic violence. The DOJ is also working with state and local law enforcement groups and United States Attorneys on effective implementation of this law.

As set forth below, the first successful prosecution under the Act's firearms disability provision occurred in South Dakota.

On October 18, 1994, a South Dakota court issued the estranged wife of Robert M. Goben a restraining order against her husband which prohibited him from harassing or threatening her. Under the firearms disability provision of the newly enacted Crime Bill, Mr. Goben was also prohibited from possessing a firearm while the restraining order remained in effect.

Approximately five months later, while the restraining order was still in effect, local police discovered that Mr. Goben possessed a loaded .22-caliber magnum revolver. As a result, Mr. Goben was arrested and pled guilty to illegally possessing a firearm in violation of federal law. Mr. Goben was sentenced to twelve months in prison followed by two years of supervised release, during which time he was prohibited from contacting his former spouse.

Following the Goben case, federal prosecutors in the Northern District of Iowa brought another case under the new federal law.

On October 24, 1995, Shawn A. Hungate, 25, of Fort Dodge, Iowa, was charged with illegally possessing a firearm while subject to a restraining order. According to the complaint, when purchasing the firearm, Hungate allegedly answered "No" to a question on a government form regarding whether he was subject to a restraining order. If convicted on the firearms charge, Mr. Hungate faces up to ten years in prison and a $250,000 fine or both.

The firearms disability provision provides some measure of security to victims in that their abusers can be arrested if they attempt to purchase or possess firearms during the period of the restraining order. The DOJ is working with state and local law enforcement groups to implement this provision.

In addition, the FBI is creating a national database concerning persons subject to protection orders, which will be available for criminal justice purposes, and to civil courts in domestic violence cases. This database will increase the ability of states to verify the existence of restraining orders throughout the United States.

Mandatory Arrest Policies

Police officers have historically been reluctant to become involved in domestic violence disputes, largely because such calls for police assistance are among the most complex, emotionally charged and potentially dangerous calls to which police respond.

Many jurisdictions have implemented mandatory arrest policies. A mandatory arrest policy requires police to arrest a domestic assault offender whenever the officer determines that a crime has been committed and probable cause for arrest exists. Currently, 27 states and the District of Columbia have adopted mandatory arrest policies. These policies convey a message to the victim, the family, and the community that domestic violence is a serious crime that will not be tolerated.

The primary goal of these policies, and the immediate and primary responsibility of the arresting officer, must be to ensure the safety of the victim. The arrest of the abuser does not guarantee their safety. It has been recognized that a strong mandatory arrest policy must be supported by a community and criminal justice system which also takes a strong stand against domestic violence and makes every attempt to provide safety for the victim once an arrest is made.

The DOJ's Grants to Encourage Arrest Policies, a new program funded in 1996, helps states, localities and tribal governments treat domestic violence as a serious criminal offense. Law enforcement officers are being trained to identify patterns of abuse, and to provide the immediate support and protection a domestic violence victim requires, including shelter and counseling, medical care, and legal assistance.

Rural Domestic Violence and Child Abuse Enforcement

If a domestic violence victim in a rural area of this country needs assistance, she may be faced with many difficulties. Very few police officers patrol in small rural communities, therefore, it may be too late once a call for assistance is answered. In addition, there is understandable fear that any report of abuse will not remain a secret in small communities.

Geographic isolation, culturally close communities, and lack of domestic violence information and services are among the problems unique to rural areas. Victims in rural areas also may not trust those outside their communities to protect them from their abusers. Therefore, they may elect to continue living in emotional isolation rather than seek help. Because rural areas in the United States are also experiencing growth in their immigrant populations, victims may be further isolated as a result of language and cultural barriers.

The VAWA has established monetary grant programs which address the issues of domestic violence and child abuse in rural states. These grants are designed to: (i) create training programs for those most likely to be in contact with domestic violence victims, such as law enforcement, shelter workers, health care providers, and clergy; (ii) increase public awareness and implement community education campaigns; and (iii) expand direct services for rural and Native American victims and their children.

A variety of entities, including states, tribal and local governments, and public and private organizations in rural states, are eligible to receive funding under the grant programs.

Community Oriented Policing Services ("COPS")

As part of the VAWA, the "COPS" (Community Oriented Policing Services) Office was established with a mission to place an additional 100,000 law enforcement officers on the nation's street in order to promote community policing. The COPS' Community Policing to Combat Domestic Violence Program provides law enforcement agencies with an opportunity to implement innovative strategies utilizing community policing to deal with domestic violence.

To be eligible for funding under this program, police departments and sheriffs' offices are required to collaborate with non-profit, non-governmental victim service programs, domestic violence shelters, or community service groups to coordinate efforts to fight domestic abuse. As a few jurisdictions have already found, community policing—a strategy which emphasizes problem solving and community partnership—can be an effective weapon in decreasing the incidence of domestic violence.

For example, efforts have been made to educate and involve the public on ways they can help to diminish domestic violence. Individuals who come in contact with suspected domestic abuse are advised not to ignore the situation. If a violent incident is witnessed or overheard, one should contact the police immediately. Medical providers and clergy members should make further inquiries when evidence of domestic violence are present, and teachers must watch for signs that children have witnessed violence in the home, such as violent tendencies exhibited by the child.

As the case below demonstrates, a successful end to domestic violence can only be accomplished if a coordinated effort is made by all individuals who come in contact with domestic abuse.

In 1992, a 39 year old Alexandria, Virginia woman went to the hospital with a black eye and cuts which required stitches. She told the nurse that her husband had caused her injuries, but asked the nurse not to call the police because she feared retaliation from her husband.

The nurse did not comply with the woman's wishes and called the police to report the abuse. Once the police came, they enabled the victim to get help. The husband was charged with abuse, and the woman was given lodging and counseling at a shelter for battered women.

Armed with advice concerning her legal rights, the woman was able to obtain a protective order from the court which allowed her to return to her apartment and prohibited her husband from returning. The court ordered the husband into an anger management program.

This woman credits that nurse's intervention, although against her wishes, with freeing her from the violent relationship when she did not have the courage to leave on her own.

Strategies for the Domestic Violence Victim

It is important for women who are in abusive relationships to recognize the risk factors, and to prepare themselves for the possibility of flight in case the situation becomes dangerous. The following advice and information has been gathered from nationwide domestic violence organizations, such as the National Victim Center, in order to give the domestic violence victim some coping strategies at various stages of a domestic violence relationship.

Risk Factors for Abusive Behavior

Research has indicated a number of identifying factors which place a man at risk as a potential batterer, including: (i) unemployment; (ii) poverty; (iii) drug or alcohol use; (iv) witnessing spousal abuse among parents as a child; (v) lack of education; and (vi) age 18 to 30 years old.

A recent study suggests that possessiveness is the most prevalent reason given by male offenders for killing their partners, and spousal homicide occurs more frequently during a period when the couple are separated, particularly if the separation was initiated by the wife.

Strategies While Still in the Abusive Relationship

Of course, a victim of domestic violence is advised to immediately leave the abusive relationship to avoid serious personal injury to herself or the children. Nevertheless, it is recognized that many women, for whatever reason, try to endure the violent behavior for as long as possible. In those cases, the following advice should be heeded:

1. If it appears that abuse is about to occur, don't be combative. Try to diffuse the situation by backing down or leaving the situation to allow your partner to cool off.

2. Prepare safety areas in your home where you can go if you must escape abuse. Keep all types of weapons, if any, locked up in a remote location. If an abusive situation appears imminent, go to the safety area. Maintain a phone in that area in case you need to call for help. Try to remember a list of important phone numbers, such as the police, ambulance, shelter, and hotline numbers, including the national domestic violence hotline number which is further discussed below.

3. If you have children, try to stay away from them during an abusive episode so that they do not also become targets of the abuser.

4. If you are unable to avoid the violent attack, protect vulnerable areas of your body,—e.g. your head and face—by blocking with your arms.

5. Don't hide your situation from family and close friends. You may have to rely on them for help if the situation gets really out of hand.

6. Teach your children how to get help if the need arises. Caution them not to involve themselves in the altercation. Explain to them that violence is wrong, and they are not at fault.

Making Plans to Leave the Abusive Relationship

If the relationship becomes too turbulent and unpredictable to endure, the domestic violence victim must make plans to leave the situation. In that case, the following advice should be heeded.

1. Maintain a journal of all of the violent incidents, and keep it and any evidence of physical abuse, such as photographs, in a safe place where you will have access to them after you leave.

2. If you are injured, seek medical care at the emergency room of a hospital or your physician. Make sure your account of the injuries is documented.

3. Contact your local battered women's shelter for information about your legal rights, sources of financial assistance, counseling and other available resources. Again, the national domestic violence hotline is also equipped to provide resource information to victims.

4. If you are unemployed, seek out job training and educational programs to help prepare you for entering the workforce.

5. Practice an escape plan in case the need arises. Plan for all possible contingencies. For example, get into the habit of having your car ready for emergency departures and a spare set of keys in case yours are confiscated. Hide some emergency money, and keep a suitcase packed with some essential clothing and supplies for yourself and your children.

Leaving the Abusive Relationship

1. Ask the police to accompany you while you remove your personal belongings from the home and to escort you from the home.

2. Make sure you take with you important items that you will need and may not want to risk reentering the home to retrieve, such as your drivers license; legal documents, such as your marriage license, birth certificates, citizenship documents and social security cards; banking information and checkbook; property ownership documents, such as titles and deeds; credit cards; medical records and prescription medication; school records; insurance information; personal valuables and effects; and your personal telephone book with important phone numbers.

3. Try to create a false trail so that the abuser cannot easily track you down. Don't use calling card numbers that can be traced back to your whereabouts. Don't use credit cards in areas that you intend to relocate.

After you successfully leave the violent relationship, seek advice from domestic violence organizations on how to proceed to protect yourself and your children from further abuse. Court intervention may be necessary. In extreme cases, relocation may be the only alternative.

The National Domestic Violence Hotline

In 1996, as authorized by the VAWA, President Clinton announced the implementation of a nationwide, 24-hour toll-free domestic violence hotline. This hotline is the first federally funded national domestic violence hotline in this country.

Under the VAWA, the Department of Health and Human Services was authorized to provide a $1 million grant to establish the hotline, with an additional $400,000 in annual funding to maintain the service for the following five years. Private donations also help fund the hotline.

The hotline provides help for domestic violence victims across the country—24-hours a day, 365 days a year. The service is toll-free, operating throughout the United States, Puerto Rico, and the Virgin Islands.

The hotline is designed to help create a more unified system among local, state, and national service providers. Although there are already a number of local domestic violence hotlines in place, many areas in this country still lack a comprehensive response system. The national hotline is especially important for victims who live in rural or isolated areas which may lack their own local hotlines or other comprehensive domestic violence services.

When someone calls the hotline, they speak to a trained domestic violence advocate, who offers them crisis intervention, support, and referrals to local services in their community. The advocate has access to a national database that contains the most current information on emergency shelters, legal advocacy, social services, and other programs in communities across the country. In an emergency, the hotline is also equipped to connect callers to their local police. Services are also available to the hearing impaired, and translators are available for non-English speaking victims of domestic violence.

The National Domestic Violence Hotline can be reached at 1-800-799-SAFE. The TDD number for the hearing impaired is 1-800-787-3224. It is important to note that callers who need help in an emergency should always call "911" directly for immediate assistance.

Resource directories of national, state and regional domestic violence organizations, and of organizations which provide advice and services to women victims of violent crime are set forth in Appendices 9, 10, 11 and 12.

CHAPTER 4:

SEXUAL ASSAULT

In General

Sexual assault is a general term which refers to a number of sex-related offenses, including rape, sexual contact, and indecent exposure. Sexual assault involves the commission of those acts against another who is either unwilling to consent, or who lacks the physical, mental or legal capacity to consent, e.g. a minor. The crime of sexual assault almost always involves sexual intercourse, including oral or anal intercourse, or some other type of penetration of the genitals by another's body or by an object.

Statistics

According to the Department of Justice Bureau of Justice Statistics ("BJS"), in 1995, victims reported an estimated 260,310 completed or attempted rapes and 94,580 sexual assaults. The Federal Bureau of Investigation ("FBI") further reports that, in 1995, one forcible rape occurred every five minutes.

The profile of the most likely victim of rape or sexual assault is a female, between the ages of 16 and 19, who lives in an urban center and comes from a low income household. Although the victims of sexual assault are primarily female, many states have recently amended their laws to make such crimes gender-neutral.

Burden of Proof

In prosecuting a sexual assault case, the issue of consent is of primary importance. If the victim was acquainted with the offender—e.g. date rape—it often becomes a matter of credibility unless there is further corroborating evidence, such as witnesses. However, some states have passed laws prohibiting law enforcement officers from requiring the victim of a sexual assault to submit to a polygraph test as a condition of beginning the criminal investigation.

In addition, most states no longer require evidence that the victim attempted to physically resist the attacker, and in all 50 states, it is now a crime to sexually assault one's spouse.

Rape Shield Laws

The defense usually attempts to undermine the sex crime victim's credibility by exploring the victim's sexual history and reputation. It is because of this embarrassment that the majority of sexual assaults go unreported to police. Over the last two decades, many states have passed laws to reform the procedures for prosecuting sexual assault so that permissible evidence focuses on the specific facts of the alleged assault, rather than the victim's past sexual conduct. In fact, most states have passed legislation—known as "rape shield" laws—which prohibits the introduction of the victim's past sexual history into evidence.

In addition to these state laws, Section 40141 of the Safe Streets for Women provision of the VAWA amended the Federal Rules of Evidence to prohibit the admission of evidence offered to prove: (i) that a victim engaged in other sexual behavior; or (ii) a victim's alleged sexual predisposition.

The only exceptions to the federal rules apply in criminal cases where: (i) evidence of specific instances of sexual behavior by the victim are offered to prove that a person other than the accused was the actual perpetrator; (ii) evidence of specific instances of sexual behavior by the victim with respect to the accused are offered to prove consent; and (iii) the evidence, if excluded, would violate the defendant's constitutional rights.

In addition, in a civil case, evidence offered to prove the sexual behavior or sexual predisposition of a victim is admissible if its probative value substantially outweighs the danger of harm to any victim and unfair prejudice to any party. Nevertheless, evidence of a victim's reputation is admissible only if it has been placed in controversy by the victim.

Similar Crimes Evidence in Sex Offense Cases

The 1994 Crime Bill enacted general rules of admissibility in federal sexual assault and child molestation cases for evidence that the defendant has committed other similar offenses, facilitating the effective prosecution of habitual sex offenders. The new evidence rules provide the basis for informed decisions by juries regarding questions of propensity to commit future crimes in light of the defendant's past conduct.

This amendment to the Federal Rules of Evidence serves as a model for the states, which prosecute the majority of sex offense crimes. California followed the federal example, and enacted its own evidence provision for sexual offense cases modeled after the Federal Rules. The DOJ was instrumental in the California reform by providing technical assistance and participating in the state legislative hearings.

As the facts of the following case demonstrate, reforming state evidentiary rules to admit evidence of prior sexual offenses is crucial to ensuring the safety of women and children against sexual predators.

Joey Sanza raped and murdered Theresa Cha when she came to meet her husband in the building where Mr. Sanza worked. There was extensive physical and circumstantial evidence that Mr. Sanza committed the crime. In addition, the jury was informed about three other rapes that Mr. Sanza had committed in another state.

Mr. Sanza's other sexual offenses were relevant to help confirm his identity as Theresa Cha's attacker by showing his propensity and capacity to commit sexually violent crimes.

Nevertheless, Sanza's conviction for raping and murdering Theresa Cha was reversed on appeal because the jury was told of his other crimes. People v. Sanza, 509 N.Y.S.2d 311 (App. Div. 1986).

Under the amended Federal Rules of Evidence, Mr. Sanza's conviction for rape and murder would have been upheld on appeal.

Sex Offender Registration and Community Notification

In general, sex offender registration and community notification systems assist the investigation of sex crimes by informing law enforcement authorities of the identities and whereabouts of convicted sex offenders.

These systems may also inhibit offenders—who know that the authorities know who they are and where they are—from committing additional crimes. Community notification enables communities to take common sense measures to protect themselves and their families, such as ensuring that their children do not associate or visit with known child molesters.

The Department of Justice ("DOJ") is implementing a number of provisions designed to stop sex offenders before they strike, as set forth in The Jacob Wetterling Crimes Against Children and Sexually Violent Offender Registration Act, which was strengthened by the subsequent "Megan's Law" amendment.

In addition, the DOJ has participated in state and federal litigation defending the validity of sex offender registration and notification systems in a number of jurisdictions. Most recently, it assisted in the successful defense of the validity of the New Jersey sex offender registration and notification system.

The Jacob Wetterling Crimes Against Children and Sexually Violent Offender Registration Act

The Jacob Wetterling Crimes Against Children and Sexually Violent Offender Registration Act ("The Jacob Wetterling Act") provides states with a monetary incentive to adopt effective registration systems for convicted child molesters and other persons convicted of sexually violent crimes.

Under the Act, community notification concerning the location of registered offenders is permitted where necessary for public safety. Most states have some form of sex offender registration but few regularly verify an offender's address. The Jacob Wetterling guidelines will help state law enforcement agencies communicate with each other regarding sex offenders who cross state lines.

The full text of the Jacob Wetterling Act is set forth in Appendix 13.

Megan's Law

"Megan's Law" basically requires that neighbors, community officials, organizations and individuals working with potential victims of sex offenders, e.g. children, or those likely to come in contact with the sex offender, be notified that the convicted sex offender is living amongst them. In addition, sex offenders are required to register with a state agency in order to keep track of their behavior and whereabouts.

Over 40 states have passed laws requiring the registration of sexual offenders with state agencies. This type of law has commonly been referred to as "Megan's Law" named after a child who was sexually assaulted and murdered by a convicted sexual offender who was living in her neighborhood in anonymity.

On July 29, 1994, seven-year-old Megan Kanka was sexually assaulted and murdered by a twice-convicted sex offender who moved in across the street from her family's home in New Jersey. The offender promised to show Megan his new puppy, luring her into his home where he raped and murdered her. Megan's body was subsequently found nearby.

Prior to the passage of Megan's Law, Section 170101(d) of the Jacob Wetterling Act provided that the information collected under a state sex offender registration program would be treated as private data except: (i) for disclosure to law enforcement agencies for law enforcement purposes; (ii) for disclosure to government agencies conducting confidential background checks; and (iii) that the designated state law enforcement agency and any local law enforcement agency authorized by the state shall release relevant information that is necessary to protect the public concerning a specific person required to register.

Megan's Law amended Section 170101(d) to provide that the information collected under a state sex offender registration program may be disclosed: (i) for any purpose permitted under the laws of the state; and (ii) that the designated state law enforcement agency and any local law enforcement agency authorized by the state shall release relevant information that is necessary to protect the public concerning a specific person required to register.

Thus, "Megan's Law" did away with the section that treated sex offender registration information as private, paving the way for state's to publish this information to the community.

The full text of Megan's Law is set forth in Appendix 14.

Child Rape

During 1992, 109,000 rapes were reported to law enforcement agencies by females. The BJS conducted a study of these rape victims in 11 states and the District of Columbia (the "1992 Study"). This study was the first to document the frequency of child rape. The findings are very disturbing.

According to the 1992 study, one-half of the female rape victims were under 18 years old, and sixteen percent were younger than 12 years old. During this time period, 17,000 females under the age of 12 were reportedly raped nationwide. The actual number of rapes is likely to be much higher because many victims choose not to report the crime to law enforcement authorities.

A separate BJS study of rape victims in three states—Alabama, North Dakota and South Carolina—which was conducted in 1991 (the "1991 Study"), found that 96 percent of the female rape victims younger than 12 years old knew their attackers. Only 4 percent of the rape victims younger than 12 were attacked by strangers. 50 percent of the perpetrators were friends or acquaintances, and 46 percent were family members. In fact, twenty percent of the children were victimized by their fathers.

According to a 1991 BJS survey of state prisoners convicted of raping a child under 12 years old, 94 percent of the offenders said their victim was either a family member, acquaintance or friend. This figure supports the findings of the 1991 study.

According to BJS statistics, it appears that as the age of the female increases, rape by a family member decreases dramatically, while the incidence of rape by a stranger rises.

For example, among female victims aged 12 to 17, 20 percent were raped by family members, 65 percent by an acquaintance or friend and 15 percent by a stranger. Among female victims age 18 years or older, 12 percent were raped by a family member, 55 percent by an acquaintance or friend and 33 percent by a stranger.

Confidential Communications for Rape Victims

Unfortunately, when a woman who has been victimized by sexual assault reports the crime and seeks help through counseling, she all too often finds herself victimized again when the attorney defending the sex offender issues subpoenas for her counseling records. Because many sexual assault and domestic violence counselors are not psychologists or psychotherapists, they cannot claim that such communications are privileged under many state statutes.

In order to encourage victims of sexual assault to report the crimes, the victims must be able to communicate freely and confidentially with their counselors. Without this guarantee of confidentiality, sexual assault and domestic violence victims will continue to be reluctant to report these serious crimes, and will avoid seeking necessary crisis intervention and counseling.

Under the VAWA, the DOJ is required to study and evaluate the manner in which states have taken steps to protect the confidentiality of communications between sexual assault victims and their counselors, and to develop model legislation which protects such communication.

To date, 27 states and the District of Columbia have enacted statutes that protect these confidential communications. In those states where such communications are not protected, the DOJ's mission is to disseminate model legislation and encourage those states to adopt legislation.

Establishing statutory testimonial privileges for sexual assault and domestic violence counselors will help ensure that these important communications will remain confidential and that victims will not be reluctant to report the crimes and seek help.

Rape-Related Post-Traumatic Stress Disorder (RR-PTSD)

According to the National Victim Center, nearly one-third of all rape victims develop what is known as Rape-related Post-traumatic Stress Disorder (RR-PTSD) at some point in their life following the attack.

The first symptom of RR-PTSD is the feeling of reliving the traumatic experience. This occurs when the victim is unable to block out remembrances—e.g. flashbacks—about the rape incident. There are often accompanying nightmares in which the victim relives the whole experience. In addition, the victim often feels overwhelming distress when confronted with stimuli which symbolize the trauma.

Another major symptom of RR-PTSD is social withdrawal, also referred to as "psychogenic numbing," which leaves the victim feeling emotionally dead. The victim no longer experiences normal feelings such as those felt prior to the traumatic incident. For example, victims may no longer feel the normal range of human emotions, such as happiness and sorrow. Survivors of crime victims may also experience a decreased interest in living.

The victim is also likely to develop a form of amnesia concerning the details of the experience. This is a defense mechanism which takes over to protect the victim from experiencing further psychic trauma.

A third major symptom of RR-PTSD involves avoidance behavior. Avoidance behavior occurs when the victim attempts to avoid any thoughts, feelings or contacts which might stimulate a remembrance of the trauma. For example, a rape victim may refuse to drive in the area close to where the sexual assault occurred.

The fourth set of symptoms include an exaggerated startle response, inability to sleep, memory impairment, and difficulty concentrating. Victims may also exhibit episodes of anger and irritability which have no identifiable cause. Rape victims are three times more likely to suffer major depressive episodes as compared to those who have not been victimized. In addition, rape victims are 4.1 times more likely to contemplate suicide, and thirteen percent actually follow through with a suicide attempt. Some also develop drug and alcohol problems following the traumatic experience.

Sexually Transmitted Disease

An additional factor in the psychological trauma associated with sexual assault is the fear that the victim has been exposed to a sexually transmitted disease and, in particular, to the potentially deadly and widespread HIV infection.

According to statistics gathered by the Center for Disease Control (CDC) in 1994, there had been 441,528 documented cases of AIDS, of which 270,870 infected individuals have already died. The CDC estimates that by the year 2000, approximately 100 million adults and 10 million children will be infected worldwide.

The incidence of HIV infection is so pervasive that most citizens knows of at least one infected person. It is no wonder that victims of sexual assault are concerned about potential exposure. The fear is real and greatly exacerbates the stress a victim of sexual assault is already caused to endure.

Following the assault, the victim must make the decision on whether to be tested. It is recommended that the victim receive counseling both before and after being tested. If they wish to be tested, it is important that the test be taken as soon after the assault as possible for a baseline reading.

If the test results are negative, it is suggested that additional testing take place every six months for the following eighteen months. Of course, if the test results are positive, the impact will be devastating and intensive counseling will be required.

Nevertheless, the victim should be aware that a positive HIV test does not mean he or she has, or will develop, full-blown AIDS. Further, medical treatment has advanced to the point where death is not imminent, and some HIV infected individuals experience little, if any, symptoms.

Treatment for Sex Offenders

The VAWA requires the Attorney General to ensure that relevant sex offender treatment information is provided to sex offenders prior to their release from prison. The Bureau of Prisons ("BOP") has coordinated these efforts with two offender treatment program information clearinghouses in the United States. The BOP, together with the U.S. Probation Office, is also ensuring that released sex offenders follow-up with community-based treatment.

CHAPTER 5:

STALKING

In General

The term "stalking" describes any unwanted contact by an individual—referred to as a "stalker"—and his or her victim, which places the victim in fear for his or her safety. However, the legal definition of stalking varies according to state law, which may specifically define prohibited stalking behavior.

The act of stalking is not new. It is essentially conduct which was previously described as a form of harassment. The victims—usually women—are followed, harassed, and threatened by offenders who are usually the victim's former husband or boyfriend. Only recently has stalking been categorized as a separate offense, in large part due to the number of high-profile celebrity victims who have been subjected to stalking.

It is estimated that approximately 200,000 citizens are currently being stalked, and that 1 in 20 women will be stalked at least one time during their life.

Legislation

In 1990, California became the first state to pass a law which specifically defined stalking as a crime. This action was taken in response to several cases in which stalking victims were eventually murdered. These victims had previously tried to make complaints to the police about the stalking behavior, however, the existing law required that the offender take some affirmative action before they could make an arrest. This requirement was changed with the new stalking law, permitting police to intervene at an earlier stage.

As of 1993, all states and the District of Columbia had enacted some type of anti-stalking legislation. Although the specific provisions may vary state by state, they all generally prohibit stalking behaviors that are intimidating and place the victim in fear for his or her safety. The reader is advised to check the law of his or her own jurisdiction for specific provisions of that state's stalking law.

In addition, a number of criminal justice and victims' rights organizations have since promulgated a model stalking statute, and a recently enacted federal law prohibits an individual from crossing state lines for the purposes of stalking his or her victim.

Subtitle F of the VAWA, entitled National Stalker and Domestic Violence Reduction, addresses the problem of stalking. Section 40601 authorizes access to information from national crime information databases consisting of identification records, criminal history records, protection orders and wanted person records by civil or criminal courts in connection with stalking or domestic violence cases.

In addition, this section authorizes federal and state criminal justice agencies to enter information into the criminal information database concerning individuals who have been arrested or convicted on stalking charges, or for whom arrest warrants or protection orders for stalking are pending.

The Act also provides monetary grants to states and local governmental units to establish programs and improve procedures for entering data regarding stalking and domestic violence incidents into local, state and national crime information databases.

Proof

Although stalking laws no longer require the victim to wait until the stalker takes some affirmative action, the victim is still required to provide sufficient evidence to establish probable cause that the perpetrator engaged in illegal conduct. The victim is advised to keep a journal documenting each stalking incident. Photographs and videotapes, voice mail messages, correspondence and witness affidavits are types of evidence that may be used to establish probable cause.

Profile of a Stalker

Although most stalkers are male, a stalker can be any gender. A stalking victim can be either male or female, however, most victims are female. Stalkers come from all types of backgrounds. Because this phenomenon has only recently been subjected to scientific study, clearcut psychological profiles have not yet been determined. However, forensic psychologists generally place stalkers in one of two broad categories: (i) Love Obsession Stalkers; and (ii) Simple Obsession Stalkers.

Love Obsession Stalkers

A love obsession stalker is one who becomes fixated on an individual with whom they have no relationship, e.g. a total stranger or someone who they barely know. The stalkers who stalk celebrities fall into this category, which accounts for approximately one-fourth of all stalking behavior.

Psychologists believe that most love obsession stalkers suffer from schizophrenia or paranoia which is manifested in delusional thoughts and behavior. Their inability to function normally in relationships causes them to create a fantasy life in which their victim plays an important role as their love interest. They then proceed to try and live out this fantasy life.

Of course, the victims are unaware of their role in this obsession, and are unwilling to participate. In turn, this causes the stalker concern as he or she tries to make the victim conform to his or her role. The stalker may resort to threats, intimidation, and even violence, so that their fantasy can be brought to fruition.

Simple Obsession Stalkers

A simple obsession stalker is one who is obsessed with an individual with whom they had a previous personal relationship. This category makes up the majority of stalking behavior. The simple obsession stalker is commonly an ex-husband or mate who desires to control his former partner. "Fatal attraction" stalkers—individuals who become obsessed during a casual short-term relationship—also fall under this category.

Simple obsession stalkers generally do not have a mental disorder as do love obsession stalkers, however, psychologists do believe these individuals suffer serious personality disorders, similar to those exhibited by physical abusers in domestic violence situations.

The characteristics which appear to be common to all simple obsession stalkers, include: (i) the inability to maintain relationships; (ii) extreme jealousy and possessiveness; (iii) emotional immaturity and insecurity; (iv) low self-esteem; and (v) the need to control their partners through intimidation and/or violence.

Thus, once their partner leaves, this rejection causes their self-esteem to plummet as they become paranoid about their loss of control over that person. They become obsessed with regaining possession and total control over their former mate. If they are unable to do so, they often resort to violence—e.g., "if I can't have him/her, nobody else will." In fact, there is a very high incidence of spousal murder associated with domestic violence victims who decide to leave their partners.

Nevertheless, the behavior of stalkers is often unpredictable. That is what makes the crime so dangerous. The perpetrator may be sending love letters and roses one day, and the following day physically assault the object of their obsession. Conversely, the stalker may engage in non-threatening stalking behavior for many, many months without ever escalating to a more aggressive stage.

Safety Strategies for Stalking Victims

A stalking victim who is being subjected to particularly threatening behavior should go to the nearest police station and immediately report the crime. If it is not possible to find a nearby police station at the time, safety may be sought at a church, shelter or other public place where a stalker is less likely to make a scene. Until the situation is brought under control, the stalking victim may consider relocating to a location where he or she will not be found.

If the danger is not imminent, but the potential for violence is there, a stalking victim should consider petitioning the court for an order of protection, as discussed in Chapter 3 of this almanac. Again, however, the reader is cautioned that an order of protection is merely a piece of paper, and will not stop a perpetrator who is intent on harming his or her victim.

CHAPTER 6:

BATTERED IMMIGRANT WOMEN AND CHILDREN

In General

Subtitle G of the Violence Against Women Act of 1994 ("VAWA"), entitled Protections for Battered Immigrant Women and Children, provides certain statutory protection to battered immigrant women and their children, thus permitting them to petition for classification and/or avoid deportation.

It should be noted that, although this provision specifically addresses battered immigrant "women," abused spouses and children of either sex may benefit from these provisions.

It has been recognized that some immigrant women and children who are battered face unique obstacles. In addition to the physical violence, the threat of deportation or release of information about legal status has been used against these women by their violent mates as a means to instill fear and dependency in order to keep the abused person in the violent relationship.

Prior to the new federal statute, immigrant spouses were dependent on their citizen or permanent resident spouses to petition on their behalf for permanent resident status. This threat of denying classification was often a sword held over the heads of these women by their abusive mates as a control mechanism.

The Immigration and Naturalization Service ("INS") has finalized regulations to implement the new federal statute, thus establishing the procedures for self-petitioning by the abused spouse. Under the new law, battered immigrant women are able to file their own petitions for lawful permanent resident status for themselves and for their children, without the knowledge or consent of the abuser.

Changes in the abuser's citizenship or lawful permanent resident status will not affect the validity of an approved self-petition. This regulatory provision eliminates the possibility that an abuser could recapture control over the abused spouse's immigration classification by changing his or her own immigration status.

Further, an approved self-petition will not be revoked solely because the abuser subsequently abandons lawful permanent resident status, renounces United States citizenship, is deported, or otherwise changes immigration status.

Eligibility for Self-Petitioning

Under the law, a qualified spouse or child is entitled to self-petition for immigrant classification based on their relationship to the abusive citizen or lawful permanent resident of the United States, and further allows certain abused spouses and children who have been continuously physically present in the United States for the past 3 years to apply for suspension of deportation.

A spouse who is self-petitioning for immigrant classification must show that:

1. She is the spouse of a citizen or lawful permanent resident of the United States;

2. She is eligible for immigrant classification under section 201(b)(2)(A)(i) or 203(a)(2)(A) of the INA based on that relationship;

3. She resides in the United States;

4. She has resided in the United States with the citizen or lawful permanent resident spouse;

5. She has been battered by, or has been the subject of extreme cruelty perpetrated by, the citizen or lawful permanent resident during the marriage; or is the parent of a child who has been battered by, or has been the subject of extreme cruelty perpetrated by, the citizen or lawful permanent resident during the marriage;

6. She is a person of good moral character;

7. She is a person whose deportation would result in extreme hardship to herself, or her child; and

8. She entered into the marriage to the citizen or lawful permanent resident in good faith.

Requirement of Present Marriage

The law provides that the battered spouse must be presently married to a citizen or lawful permanent resident of the United States, and includes no provisions for filing a self-petition based on a former spousal relationship. Therefore, the self-petitioning spouse must be legally married to the abuser when the petition is filed or the petition will be denied. This is so whether the marriage ended by annulment, death, or divorce before the petition was filed.

Although the law does not allow a self-petition to be filed based on a former spousal relationship, it directs the INS not to revoke approval of a self-petition solely because the marriage has legally ended. This statutory provision protects the self-petitioner against an abuser's attempt to regain control over the petitioning process through legal termination of the marriage.

Although the law requires the marriage to be legally valid at the time of filing, and specifies that its termination after approval will not be the sole basis for revocation, it does not address the effect of a legal termination occurring between the filing and the approval of the self-petition. In the absence of explicit legislative guidelines, the INS has determined that protections for spouses should be extended to cover the entire period after the self-petition is filed.

Effect of Remarriage

If the self-petitioner chooses to remarry while the petition is pending, the self-petitioner has established a new spousal relationship and has shown that he or she no longer needs the protections of the law to equalize the balance of power in the relationship with the abuser. Thus, the petition will be denied.

However, if the new husband or wife is a citizen or lawful permanent resident of the United States, he or she may file for the former self-petitioner's classification as an immigrant. The self-petitioner also would not be precluded from filing a self-petition based on the new family relationship if the new spouse is an abusive citizen or lawful permanent resident of the United States.

Evidence of Marriage

Primary evidence of a marital relationship is a marriage certificate issued by civil authorities and proof of the termination of all prior marriages, if any, of both the self-petitioner and the abuser.

Primary evidence of the abuser's U.S. citizenship or lawful permanent residence is:

1. A birth certificate issued by a civil authority establishing the abuser's birth in the United States;

2. The abuser's unexpired full-validity United States passport;

3. A statement issued by a U.S. consular officer certifying the abuser to be a U.S. citizen and the bearer of a currently valid U.S. passport;

4. The abuser's Certificate of Naturalization or Certificate of Citizenship;

5. A Department of State Form FS-240, Report of Birth Abroad of a Citizen of the United States, relating to the abuser; or

6. The abuser's Form I-151 or Form I-551 Alien Registration Receipt Card, or other proof given by the Service as evidence of lawful permanent residence.

If primary or secondary evidence of an abuser's immigration or citizenship status is not available, this rule provides that the INS will attempt to electronically verify the abuser's status from information contained in INS computerized records. Other INS records may also be reviewed at the discretion of the adjudicating officer.

Marriage Fraud

Self-petitioners are subject to certain provisions of the Immigration Marriage Fraud Amendments of 1986 (IMFA), which were enacted by Congress to detect and deter immigration-related marriage fraud. Thus, a petition must be denied under the provisions of section 204(c) of the INA if there is substantial and probative evidence that the self-petitioner has ever attempted or conspired to enter into a marriage for the purpose of evading the immigration laws.

The self-petitioner need not have been convicted of, or even prosecuted for, the attempt or conspiracy, nor is it necessary for the self-petitioner to have received a benefit thereby. The mere evidence of the attempt or conspiracy must be contained in the self-petitioner's immigration file.

In addition, Section 204(g) of the INA prohibits the approval of a self-petition if the marriage creating the relationship to the citizen or permanent resident took place while the self-petitioner was in deportation, exclusion, or related proceedings, unless the self-petitioner provides clear and convincing evidence that the marriage was not entered into for the purpose of obtaining immigration benefits.

Residence in the United States with the Abuser

The law requires that the self-petitioner resided with the abuser in the United States. A self-petition will not be approved if the self-petitioner is not living in the United States or has never lived with the abuser in the United States. Under the provisions of this rule, however, the self-petitioner is not required to be residing with the abuser when the petition is filed.

"Residence" is defined in section 101(a)(33) of the INA as a person's general place of abode. It is also described as a person's principal, actual dwelling place in fact, without regard to intent. A self-petitioner cannot meet the residency requirements by merely visiting the United States or visiting the abuser's home in the United States while continuing to maintain a general place of abode or principal dwelling place elsewhere.

However, the self-petitioner is not required to have lived in the United States or with the abuser in the United States for any specific length of time. A qualified self-petitioner may have moved to the United States only recently, made any number of trips abroad, or resided with the abuser in the United States for only a short time.

Evidence of residency with the abuser in the United States may take many forms, including:

(i) employment records;

(ii) utility receipts;

(iii) school records;

(iv) hospital or medical records;

(v) birth certificates of children born to the spouses in the United States;

(vi) deeds, mortgages, and leases; and

(vii) insurance policies.

A self-petitioner may also submit affidavits to establish residency with the abuser. Self-petitioners who file affidavits are encouraged to provide the affidavits of more than one person. Other types of evidence may also be submitted as the INS will consider any relevant credible evidence.

Evidence of Battery or Extreme Cruelty

The law requires a self-petitioning spouse to have been battered by, or been the subject of extreme cruelty perpetrated by, the citizen or lawful permanent resident spouse; or to be the parent of a child who was battered by, or who was the subject of extreme cruelty perpetrated by, the citizen or lawful permanent resident during the marriage.

This law further specifies that only certain types of abuse will qualify a spouse to self-petition. The qualifying abuse must have taken place during the marriage to the abuser. Battery or extreme cruelty that happened at other times is not qualifying abuse. However, there is no limit on the time that may have elapsed since the last incident of qualifying abuse occurred.

The qualifying abuse also must have been committed by the abusive citizen or lawful permanent resident spouse or parent. Battery or extreme cruelty committed by any other person is not qualifying abuse, unless it can be shown that the citizen or lawful permanent resident willfully condoned or participated in the abuse.

The law provides that evidence of abuse may include, but is not limited to reports and affidavits from police, judges and other court officials, medical personnel, school officials, clergy, social workers, and other social service agency personnel.

Persons who have obtained an order of protection against the abuser or taken other legal steps to end the abuse are strongly encouraged to submit documentation. Evidence that the abuse victim sought refuge in a battered women's shelter may also be relevant. In addition, photographs of the injuries sustained by the self-petitioner, supported by affidavits, would be credible evidence.

Requirement of Good Moral Character

The law requires all self-petitioners to be persons of good moral character, and requires self-petitioning spouses to provide evidence showing that they have been persons of good moral character for the 3 years immediately preceding the date the self-petition is filed.

The law does not preclude the INS from choosing to examine the self-petitioner's conduct and acts prior to that period if there is reason to believe that the self-petitioner may not have been a person of good moral character in the past. The law provides that a self-petition may be denied or revoked if evidence establishing that the person lacks good moral character is contained in the INS file.

Derivative Children

The law allows any child of a self-petitioning spouse to be derivatively included in the self-petition, if the child has not been classified as an immigrant based on his or her own self-petition.

No separate petition is necessary for derivative classification, and the child is not required to have been the victim of abuse. The derivative child also does not need to have lived in the United States or to otherwise satisfy the criteria for filing a self-petition. The child must, however, meet the requirements for immigrant visa issuance abroad or adjustment of status in the United States.

In addition, the derivative child need not be the child of the abuser, but must qualify as the self-petitioning spouse's child under the definition of "child" contained in section 101(b)(1) of the INA. The statutory definition includes certain children born in or out of wedlock, and certain legitimated, adopted, and stepchildren.

The law also requires a child to be unmarried and less than 21 years old. A derivative son or daughter who is married or more than 21 years old will not be issued an immigrant visa or granted adjustment of status as a derivative child.

APPENDICES

APPENDIX 1:

SUBTITLE A—SAFE STREETS FOR WOMEN

SECTION 40101. SHORT TITLE.

This subtitle may be cited as the "Safe Streets for Women Act of1994'.

CHAPTER 1—FEDERAL PENALTIES FOR SEX CRIMES

SECTION 40111. REPEAT OFFENDERS.

(a) IN GENERAL- Chapter 109A of title 18, United States Code, is amended by adding at the end the following new section:

"Section 224. Repeat offenders.

"Any person who violates a provision of this chapter, after one or more prior convictions for an offense punishable under this chapter, or after one or more prior convictions under the laws of any State relating to aggravated sexual abuse, sexual abuse, or abusive sexual contact have become final, is punishable by a term of imprisonment up to twice that otherwise authorized.".

(b) AMENDMENT OF SENTENCING GUIDELINES- The Sentencing Commission shall implement the amendment made by subsection (a) by promulgating amendments, if appropriate, in the sentencing guidelines applicable to chapter 109A offenses.

SECTION 40112. FEDERAL PENALTIES.

(a) AMENDMENT OF SENTENCING GUIDELINES- Pursuant to its authority under section 994(p) of title 28, United States Code, the United States Sentencing Commission shall review and amend, where necessary, its sentencing guidelines on aggravated sexual abuse under section 2241 of title 18, United States Code, or sexual abuse under section 2242 of title 18, United States Code, as follows:

(1) The Commission shall review and promulgate amendments to the guidelines, if appropriate, to enhance penalties if more than 1 offender is involved in the offense.

(2) The Commission shall review and promulgate amendments to the guidelines, if appropriate, to reduce unwarranted disparities between the sentences for sex offenders who are known to the victim and sentences for sex offenders who are not known to the victim.

(3) The Commission shall review and promulgate amendments to the guidelines to enhance penalties, if appropriate, to render Federal penalties on Federal territory commensurate with penalties for similar offenses in the States.

(4) The Commission shall review and promulgate amendments to the guidelines, if appropriate, to account for the general problem of recidivism in cases of sex offenses, the severity of the offense, and its devastating effects on survivors.

(b) REPORT- Not later than 180 days after the date of enactment of this Act, the United States Sentencing Commission shall review and submit to Congress a report containing an analysis of Federal rape sentencing, accompanied by comment from independent experts in the field, describing—

(1) comparative Federal sentences for cases in which the rape victim is known to the defendant and cases in which the rape victim is not known to the defendant;

(2) comparative Federal sentences for cases on Federal territory and sentences in surrounding States; and

(3) an analysis of the effect of rape sentences on populations residing primarily on Federal territory relative to the impact of other Federal offenses in which the existence of Federal jurisdiction depends upon the offense's being committed on Federal territory.

SECTION 40113. MANDATORY RESTITUTION FOR SEX CRIMES.

(a) SEXUAL ABUSE-

(1) IN GENERAL- Chapter 109A of title 18, United States Code, is amended by adding at the end the following new section:

"Section 2248. Mandatory restitution

"(a) IN GENERAL- Notwithstanding section 3663, and in addition to any other civil or criminal penalty authorized by law, the court shall order restitution for any offense under this chapter.

"(b) SCOPE AND NATURE OF ORDER-

"(1) DIRECTIONS- The order of restitution under this section shall direct that—

"(A) the defendant pay to the victim (through the appropriate court mechanism) the full amount of the victim's losses as determined by the court, pursuant to paragraph (3); and

"(B) the United States Attorney enforce the restitution order by all available and reasonable means.

"(2) ENFORCEMENT BY VICTIM- An order of restitution also may be enforced by a victim named in the order to receive the restitution in the same manner as a judgment in a civil action.

"(3) DEFINITION- For purposes of this subsection, the term full amount of the victim's losses' includes any costs incurred by the victim for—

"(A) medical services relating to physical, psychiatric, or psychological care;

"(B) physical and occupational therapy or rehabilitation;

"(C) necessary transportation, temporary housing, and child care expenses;

"(D) lost income;

"(E) attorneys' fees, plus any costs incurred in obtaining a civil protection order; and

"(F) any other losses suffered by the victim as a proximate result of the offense.

"(4) ORDER MANDATORY-

(A) The issuance of a restitution order under this section is mandatory.

"(B) A court may not decline to issue an order under this section because of—

"(i) the economic circumstances of the defendant; or

"(ii) the fact that a victim has, or is entitled to, receive compensation for his or her injuries from the proceeds of insurance or any other source.

"(C)(i) Notwithstanding subparagraph (A), the court may take into account the economic circumstances of the defendant in determining the manner in which and the schedule according to which the restitution is to be paid.

"(ii) For purposes of this subparagraph, the term ""economic circumstance" includes—

"(I) the financial resources and other assets of the defendant;

"(II) projected earnings, earning capacity, and other income of the defendant; and

"(III) any financial obligations of the defendant, including obligations to dependents.

"(D) Subparagraph (A) does not apply if—

"(i) the court finds on the record that the economic circumstances of the defendant do not allow for the payment of any amount of a restitution order, and do not allow for the payment of any or some portion of the amount of a restitution order in the foreseeable future (under any reasonable schedule of payments); and

"(ii) the court enters in its order the amount of the victim's losses, and provides a nominal restitution award.

"(5) MORE THAN 1 OFFENDER- When the court finds that more than 1 offender has contributed to the loss of a victim, the court may make each offender liable for payment of the full amount of restitution or may apportion liability among the offenders to reflect the level of contribution and economic circumstances of each offender.

"(6) MORE THAN 1 VICTIM- When the court finds that more than 1 victim has sustained a loss requiring restitution by an offender, the court shall order full restitution of each victim but may provide for different payment schedules to reflect the economic circumstances of each victim.

"(7) PAYMENT SCHEDULE- An order under this section may direct the defendant to make a single lump-sum payment or partial payments at specified intervals.

"(8) SETOFF- Any amount paid to a victim under this section shall be set off against any amount later recovered as compensatory damages by the victim from the defendant in—

"(A) any Federal civil proceeding; and

"(B) any State civil proceeding, to the extent provided by the law of the State.

"(9) EFFECT ON OTHER SOURCES OF COMPENSATION- The issuance of a restitution order shall not affect the entitlement of a victim to receive compensation with respect to a loss from insurance or any other source until the payments actually received by the victim under the restitution order fully compensate the victim for the loss.

"(10) CONDITION OF PROBATION OR SUPERVISED RELEASE-Compliance with a restitution order issued under this section shall be a condition of any probation or supervised release of a defendant. If an offender fails to comply with a restitution order, the court may, after a hearing, revoke probation or a term of supervised release, modify the terms or conditions of probation or a term of supervised release, or hold the defendant in contempt pursuant to section 3583(e). In determining whether to revoke probation or a term of supervised release, modify the terms or conditions of probation or supervised release or hold a defendant serving a term of supervised release in contempt, the court shall consider the defendant's employment status, earning ability and financial resources, the willfulness of the defendant's failure to comply, and any other circumstances that may have a bearing on the defendant's ability to comply.

"(c) PROOF OF CLAIM-

"(1) AFFIDAVIT- Within 60 days after conviction and, in any event, not later than 10 days prior to sentencing, the United States Attorney (or the United States Attorney's delegee), after consulting with the victim, shall prepare and file an affidavit with the court listing the amounts subject to restitution under this section. The affidavit shall be signed by the United States Attorney (or the United States Attorney's delegee) and the victim. Should the victim object to any of the information included in the affidavit, the United States Attorney (or the United States Attorney's delegee) shall advise the victim that the victim may file a separate affidavit and shall provide the victim with an affidavit form which may be used to do so.

"(2) OBJECTION- If, after the defendant has been notified of the affidavit, no objection is raised by the defendant, the amounts attested to in the affidavit filed pursuant to paragraph (1) shall be entered in the court's restitution order. If objection is raised, the court may require the victim or the United States Attorney (or the United States Attorney's delegee) to submit further affidavits or other supporting documents, demonstrating the victim's losses.

"(3) ADDITIONAL DOCUMENTATION AND TESTIMONY- If the court concludes, after reviewing the supporting documentation and considering the defendant's objections, that there is a substantial reason for doubting the authenticity or veracity of the records submitted, the court may require additional documentation or hear testimony on those questions. The privacy of any records filed, or testimony heard, pursuant to this section shall be maintained to the greatest extent possible, and such records may be filed or testimony heard in camera.

"(4) FINAL DETERMINATION OF LOSSES- If the victim's losses are not ascertainable by the date that is 10 days prior to sentencing as provided in paragraph (1), the United States Attorney (or the United States Attorney's delegee) shall so inform the court, and the court shall set a date for the final determination of the victim's losses, not to exceed 90 days after sentencing. If the victim subsequently discovers further losses, the victim shall have 60 days after discovery of those losses in which to petition the court for an amended restitution order. Such order may be granted only upon a showing of good cause for the failure to include such losses in the initial claim for restitutionary relief.

"(d) MODIFICATION OF ORDER- A victim or the offender may petition the court at any time to modify a restitution order as appropriate in view of a change in the economic circumstances of the offender.

"(e) REFERENCE TO MAGISTRATE OR SPECIAL MASTER- The court may refer any issue arising in connection with a proposed order of restitution to a magistrate or special master for proposed findings of fact and recommendations as to disposition, subject to a de novo determination of the issue by the court.

"(f) DEFINITION- For purposes of this section, the term 'victim' means the individual harmed as a result of a commission of a crime under this chapter, including, in the case of a victim who is under 18 years of age, incompetent, incapacitated, or deceased, the legal guardian of the victim or representative of the victim's estate, another family member, or any other person appointed as suitable by the court, but in no event shall the defendant be named as such representative or guardian.".

SECTION 40114. AUTHORIZATION FOR FEDERAL VICTIM'S COUNSELORS.

There are authorized to be appropriated for the United States Attorneys for the purpose of appointing Victim/Witness Counselors for the prosecution of sex crimes and domestic violence crimes where applicable (such as the District of Columbia)—

(1) $500,000 for fiscal year 1996;

(2) $500,000 for fiscal year 1997; and

(3) $500,000 for fiscal year 1998.

CHAPTER 2—LAW ENFORCEMENT AND PROSECUTION GRANTS TO REDUCE VIOLENT CRIMES AGAINST WOMEN

SECTION 40121. GRANTS TO COMBAT VIOLENT CRIMES AGAINST WOMEN.

(a) IN GENERAL- Title I of the Omnibus Crime Control and Safe Streets Act of 1968 (42 U.S.C. 3711 et seq.), as amended by section 32101(a), is amended—

(1) by redesignating part T as part U;

(2) by redesignating section 2001 as section 2101; and

(3) by inserting after part S the following new part:

"PART T—GRANTS TO COMBAT VIOLENT CRIMES AGAINST WOMEN

"SECTION 2001. PURPOSE OF THE PROGRAM AND GRANTS.

"(a) GENERAL PROGRAM PURPOSE- The purpose of this part is to assist States, Indian tribal governments, and units of local government to develop and strengthen effective law enforcement and prosecution strategies to combat violent crimes against women, and to develop and strengthen victim services in cases involving violent crimes against women.

"(b) PURPOSES FOR WHICH GRANTS MAY BE USED- Grants under this part shall provide personnel, training, technical assistance, data collection and other equipment for the more widespread apprehension, prosecution, and adjudication of persons committing violent crimes against women, and specifically, for the purposes of—

"(1) training law enforcement officers and prosecutors to more effectively identify and respond to violent crimes against women, including the crimes of sexual assault and domestic violence;

"(2) developing, training, or expanding units of law enforcement officers and prosecutors specifically targeting violent crimes against women, including the crimes of sexual assault and domestic violence;

"(3) developing and implementing more effective police and prosecution policies, protocols, orders, and services specifically devoted to preventing, identifying, and responding to violent crimes against women, including the crimes of sexual assault and domestic violence;

"(4) developing, installing, or expanding data collection and communication systems, including computerized systems, linking police, prosecutors, and courts or for the purpose of identifying and tracking arrests, protection orders, violations of protection orders, prosecutions, and convictions for violent crimes against women, includ ing the crimes of sexual assault and domestic violence;

"(5) developing, enlarging, or strengthening victim services programs, including sexual assault and domestic violence programs, developing or improving delivery of victim services to racial, cultural, ethnic, and language minorities, providing specialized domestic violence court advocates in courts where a significant number of protection orders are granted, and increasing reporting and reducing attrition rates for cases involving violent crimes against women, including crimes of sexual assault and domestic violence;

"(6) developing, enlarging, or strengthening programs addressing stalking; and

"(7) developing, enlarging, or strengthening programs addressing the needs and circumstances of Indian tribes in dealing with violent crimes against women, including the crimes of sexual assault and domestic violence.

"SECTION 2002. STATE GRANTS.

"(a) GENERAL GRANTS- The Attorney General may make grants to States, for use by States, units of local government, nonprofit nongovernmental victim services programs, and Indian tribal governments for the purposes described in section 2001(b).

"(b) AMOUNTS- Of the amounts appropriated for the purposes of this part—

"(1) 4 percent shall be available for grants to Indian tribal governments;

"(2) $500,000 shall be available for grants to applicants in each State; and

"(3) the remaining funds shall be available for grants to applicants in each State in an amount that bears the same ratio to the amount of remaining funds as the population of the State bears to the population of all of the States that results from a distribution among the States on the basis of each State's population in relation to the population of all States (not including populations of Indian tribes).

"(c) QUALIFICATION- Upon satisfying the terms of subsection (d), any State shall be qualified for funds provided under this part upon certification that—

"(1) the funds shall be used for any of the purposes described in section 2001(b);

"(2) grantees and subgrantees shall develop a plan for implementation and shall consult and coordinate with nonprofit, nongovernmental victim services programs, including sexual assault and domestic violence victim services programs;

"(3) at least 25 percent of the amount granted shall be allocated, without duplication, to each of the following 3 areas: prosecution, law enforcement, and victim services; and

"(4) any Federal funds received under this part shall be used to supplement, not supplant, non-Federal funds that would otherwise be available for activities funded under this subtitle.

"(d) APPLICATION REQUIREMENTS- The application requirements provided in section 513 shall apply to grants made under this part. In addition, each application shall include the certifications of qualification required by subsection (c), including documentation from nonprofit, nongovernmental victim services programs, describing their participation in developing the plan required by subsection (c)(2). An application shall include—

"(1) documentation from the prosecution, law enforcement, and victim services programs to be assisted, demonstrating—

"(A) need for the grant funds;

"(B) intended use of the grant funds;

"(C) expected results from the use of grant funds; and

"(D) demographic characteristics of the populations to be served, including age, marital status, disability, race, ethnicity and language background;

"(2) proof of compliance with the requirements for the payment of forensic medical exams provided in section 2005; and

"(3) proof of compliance with the requirements for paying filing and service fees for domestic violence cases provided in section 2006.

"(e) DISBURSEMENT-

"(1) IN GENERAL- Not later than 60 days after the receipt of an application under this part, the Attorney General shall—

"(A) disburse the appropriate sums provided for under this part; or

"(B) inform the applicant why the application does not conform to the terms of section 513 or to the requirements of this section.

"(2) REGULATIONS- In disbursing monies under this part, the Attorney General shall issue regulations to ensure that States will—

"(A) give priority to areas of varying geographic size with the greatest showing of need based on the availability of existing domestic violence and sexual assault programs in the population and geographic area to be served in relation to the availability of such programs in other such populations and geographic areas;

"(B) determine the amount of subgrants based on the population and geographic area to be served;

"(C) equitably distribute monies on a geographic basis including nonurban and rural areas of various geographic sizes; and

"(D) recognize and address the needs of underserved populations.

"(f) FEDERAL SHARE- The Federal share of a grant made under this subtitle may not exceed 75 percent of the total costs of the projects described in the application submitted.

"(g) INDIAN TRIBES- Funds appropriated by the Congress for the activities of any agency of an Indian tribal government or of the Bureau of Indian Affairs performing law enforcement functions on any Indian lands may be used to provide the non-Federal share of the cost of programs or projects funded under this part.

"(h) GRANTEE REPORTING-

"(1) IN GENERAL- Upon completion of the grant period under this part, a State or Indian tribal grantee shall file a performance report with the Attorney General explaining the activities carried out, which report shall include an assessment of the effectiveness of those activities in achieving the purposes of this part.

"(2) CERTIFICATION BY GRANTEE AND SUBGRANTEES- A section of the performance report shall be completed by each grantee and subgrantee that performed the direct services contemplated in the application, certifying performance of direct services under the grant.

"(3) SUSPENSION OF FUNDING- The Attorney General shall suspend funding for an approved application if—

"(A) an applicant fails to submit an annual performance report;

"(B) funds are expended for purposes other than those described in this part; or

"(C) a report under paragraph (1) or accompanying assessments demonstrate to the Attorney General that the program is ineffective or financially unsound.

"SECTION 2003. DEFINITIONS.

"In this part—

"(1) the term 'Domestic Violence' includes felony or misdemeanor crimes of violence committed by a current or former spouse of the victim, by a person with whom the victim shares a child in common, by a person who is cohabitating with or has cohabitated with the victim as a spouse, by a person similarly situated to a spouse of the victim under the domestic or family violence laws of the jurisdiction receiving grant monies, or by any other adult person against a victim who is protected from that person's acts under the domestic or family violence laws of the jurisdiction receiving grant monies;

"(2) the term 'Indian Country' has the meaning stated in section 1151 of title 18, United States Code;

"(3) the term 'Indian Tribe' means a tribe, band, pueblo, nation, or other organized group or community of Indians, including any Alaska Native village or regional or village corporation (as defined in, or established pursuant to, the Alaska Native Claims Settlement Act (43 U.S.C. 1601 et seq.)), that is recognized as eligible for the special programs and services provided by the United States to Indians because of their status as Indians;

"(4) the term 'Law Enforcement' means a public agency charged with policing functions, including any of its component bureaus (such as governmental victim services programs);

"(5) the term 'Prosecution' means any public agency charged with direct responsibility for prosecuting criminal offenders, including such agency's component bureaus (such as governmental victim services programs);

"(6) the term 'Sexual Assault' means any conduct proscribed by chapter 109A of title 18, United States Code, whether or not the conduct occurs in the special maritime and territorial jurisdiction of the United States or in a Federal prison and includes both assaults committed by offenders who are strangers to the victim and assaults committed by offenders who are known or related by blood or marriage to the victim;

"(7) the term 'Underserved Populations' includes populations underserved because of geographic location (such as rural isolation), underserved racial or ethnic populations, and populations underserved because of special needs, such as language barriers or physical disabilities; and

"(8) the term 'Victim Services' means a nonprofit, nongovernmental organization that assists domestic violence or sexual assault victims, including rape crisis centers, battered women's shelters, and other sexual assault or domestic violence programs, including nonprofit, nongovernmental organizations assisting domestic violence or sexual assault victims through the legal process.

"SECTION 2004. GENERAL TERMS AND CONDITIONS.

"(a) NONMONETARY ASSISTANCE- In addition to the assistance provided under this part, the Attorney General may request any Federal agency to use its authorities and the resources granted to it under Federal law (including personnel, equipment, supplies, facilities, and managerial, technical, and advisory services) in support of State, tribal, and local assistance efforts.

"(b) REPORTING- Not later than 180 days after the end of each fiscal year for which grants are made under this part, the Attorney

General shall submit to the Committee on the Judiciary of the House of Representatives and the Committee on the Judiciary of the Senate a report that includes, for each State and for each grantee Indian tribe—

"(1) the number of grants made and funds distributed under this part;

"(2) a summary of the purposes for which those grants were provided and an evaluation of their progress;

"(3) a statistical summary of persons served, detailing the nature of victimization, and providing data on age, sex, relationship of victim to offender, geographic distribution, race, ethnicity, language, and disability; and

"(4) an evaluation of the effectiveness of programs funded under this part.

"(c) REGULATIONS OR GUIDELINES- Not later than 120 days after the date of enactment of this part, the Attorney General shall publish proposed regulations or guidelines implementing this part. Not later than 180 days after the date of enactment, the Attorney General shall publish final regulations or guidelines implementing this part.

"SECTION 2005. RAPE EXAM PAYMENTS.

"(a) RESTRICTION OF FUNDS-

"(1) IN GENERAL- A State, Indian tribal government, or unit of local government, shall not be entitled to funds under this part unless the State, Indian tribal government, unit of local government, or another governmental entity incurs the full out-of-pocket cost of forensic medical exams described in subsection (b) for victims of sexual assault.

"(2) REDISTRIBUTION- Funds withheld from a State or unit of local government under paragraph (1) shall be distributed to other States or units of local government pro rata. Funds withheld from an Indian tribal government under paragraph (1) shall be distributed

"(b) MEDICAL COSTS- A State, Indian tribal government, or unit of local government shall be deemed to incur the full out-of-pocket cost of forensic medical exams for victims of sexual assault if any government entity—

"(1) provides such exams to victims free of charge to the victim;

"(2) arranges for victims to obtain such exams free of charge to the victims; or

"(3) reimburses victims for the cost of such exams if—

"(A) the reimbursement covers the full cost of such exams, without any deductible requirement or limit on the amount of a reimbursement;

"(B) the reimbursing governmental entity permits victims to apply for reimbursement for not less than one year from the date of the exam;

"(C) the reimbursing governmental entity provides reimbursement not later than 90 days after written notification of the victim's expense; and

"(D) the State, Indian tribal government, unit of local government, or reimbursing governmental entity provides information at the time of the exam to all victims, including victims with limited or no English proficiency, regarding how to obtain reimbursement.

"SECTION 2006. FILING COSTS FOR CRIMINAL CHARGES.

"(a) IN GENERAL- A State, Indian tribal government, or unit of local government, shall not be entitled to funds under this part unless the State, Indian tribal government, or unit of local government—

"(1) certifies that its laws, policies, and practices do not require, in connection with the prosecution of any misdemeanor or felony domestic violence offense, that the abused bear the costs associated with the filing of criminal charges against the domestic violence offender, or the costs associated with the issuance or service of a warrant, protection order, or witness subpoena; or

"(2) gives the Attorney General assurances that its laws, policies and practices will be in compliance with the requirements of paragraph (1) within the later of—

"(A) the period ending on the date on which the next session of the State legislature ends; or

"(B) 2 years.

"(b) REDISTRIBUTION- Funds withheld from a State, unit of local government, or Indian tribal government under subsection (a) shall be distributed to other States, units of local government, and Indian tribal government, respectively, pro rata.".

"PART U—TRANSITION—EFFECTIVE DATE—REPEALER

"Section 2101. Continuation of rules, authorities, and proceedings.".

(c) AUTHORIZATION OF APPROPRIATIONS- Section 1001(a) of title I of the Omnibus Crime Control and Safe Streets Act of 1968 (42 U.S.C. 3793), as amended by section 32101(d), is amended—

(1) in paragraph (3) by striking "and S" and inserting "S, and T"; and

(2) by adding at the end the following new paragraph:

"(18) There are authorized to be appropriated to carry out part T—

"(A) $26,000,000 for fiscal year 1995;

"(B) $130,000,000 for fiscal year 1996;

"(C) $145,000,000 for fiscal year 1997;

"(D) $160,000,000 for fiscal year 1998;

"(E) $165,000,000 for fiscal year 1999; and

"(F) $174,000,000 for fiscal year 2000.".

CHAPTER 3—SAFETY FOR WOMEN IN PUBLIC TRANSIT AND PUBLIC PARKS

SECTION 40131. GRANTS FOR CAPITAL IMPROVEMENTS TO PREVENT CRIME IN PUBLIC TRANSPORTATION.

(a) GENERAL PURPOSE- There is authorized to be appropriated not to exceed $10,000,000, for the Secretary of Transportation (referred to in this section as the "Secretary') to make capital grants for the prevention of crime and to increase security in existing and future public transportation systems. None of the provisions of this Act may be construed to prohibit the financing of projects under this section where law enforcement responsibilities are vested in a local public body other than the grant applicant.

(b) GRANTS FOR LIGHTING, CAMERA SURVEILLANCE, AND SECURITY PHONES-

(1) From the sums authorized for expenditure under this section for crime prevention, the Secretary is authorized to make grants and loans to States and local public bodies or agencies for the purpose of increasing the safety of public transportation by—

(A) increasing lighting within or adjacent to public transportation systems, including bus stops, subway stations, parking lots, or garages;

(B) increasing camera surveillance of areas within and adjacent to public transportation systems, including bus stops, subway stations, parking lots, or garages;

(C) providing emergency phone lines to contact law enforcement or security personnel in areas within or adjacent to public transportation systems, including bus stops, subway stations, parking lots, or garages; or

(D) any other project intended to increase the security and safety of existing or planned public transportation systems.

(2) From the sums authorized under this section, at least 75 percent shall be expended on projects of the type described in subsection (b)(1) (A) and (B).

(c) REPORTING- All grants under this section are contingent upon the filing of a report with the Secretary and the Department of Justice, Office of Victims of Crime, showing crime rates in or adjacent to public transportation before, and for a 1-year period after, the capital improvement. Statistics shall be compiled on the basis of the type of crime, sex, race, ethnicity, language, and relationship of victim to the offender.

(d) INCREASED FEDERAL SHARE- Notwithstanding any other provision of law, the Federal share under this section for each capital improvement project that enhances the safety and security of public transportation systems and that is not required by law (including any other provision of this Act) shall be 90 percent of the net project cost of the project.

(e) SPECIAL GRANTS FOR PROJECTS TO STUDY INCREASING SECURITY FOR WOMEN- From the sums authorized under this section, the Secretary shall provide grants and loans for the purpose of studying ways to reduce violent crimes against women in public transit through better design or operation of public transit systems.

(f) GENERAL REQUIREMENTS- All grants or loans provided under this section shall be subject to the same terms, conditions, requirements, and provisions applicable to grants and loans as specified in section 5321 of title 49, United States Code.

SECTION 40132. GRANTS FOR CAPITAL IMPROVEMENTS TO PREVENT CRIME IN NATIONAL PARKS.

Public Law 91-383 (16 U.S.C. 1a-1 et seq.) is amended by adding at the end the following new section:

"SECTION 13. NATIONAL PARK SYSTEM CRIME PREVENTION ASSISTANCE.

"(a) AVAILABILITY OF FUNDS- There are authorized to be appropriated out of the Violent Crime Reduction Trust Fund, not to exceed $10,000,000, for the Secretary of the Interior to take all necessary actions to seek to reduce the incidence of violent crime in the National Park System.

"(b) RECOMMENDATIONS FOR IMPROVEMENT- The Secretary shall direct the chief official responsible for law enforcement within the National Park Service to—

"(1) compile a list of areas within the National Park System with the highest rates of violent crime;

"(2) make recommendations concerning capital improvements, and other measures, needed within the National Park System to reduce the rates of violent crime, including the rate of sexual assault; and

"(3) publish the information required by paragraphs (1) and (2) in the Federal Register.

"(c) DISTRIBUTION OF FUNDS- Based on the recommendations and list issued pursuant to subsection (b), the Secretary shall distribute the funds authorized by subsection (a) throughout the National Park System. Priority shall be given to those areas with the highest rates of sexual assault.

"(d) USE OF FUNDS- Funds provided under this section may be used—

"(1) to increase lighting within or adjacent to National Park System units;

"(2) to provide emergency phone lines to contact law enforcement or security personnel in areas within or adjacent to National Park System units;

"(3) to increase security or law enforcement personnel within or adjacent to National Park System units; or

"(4) for any other project intended to increase the security and safety of National Park System units.".

SECTION 40133. GRANTS FOR CAPITAL IMPROVEMENTS TO PREVENT CRIME IN PUBLIC PARKS.

Section 6 of the Land and Water Conservation Fund Act of 1965 (16 U.S.C. 460 l -8) is amended by adding at the end the following new subsection:

"(h) CAPITAL IMPROVEMENT AND OTHER PROJECTS TO REDUCE CRIME-

"(1) AVAILABILITY OF FUNDS- In addition to assistance for planning projects, and in addition to the projects identified in subsection (e), and from amounts appropriated out of the Violent Crime Reduction Trust Fund, the Secretary may provide financial assistance to the States, not to exceed $15,000,000, for projects or combinations thereof for the purpose of making capital improvements and other measures to increase safety in urban parks and recreation areas, including funds to—

"(A) increase lighting within or adjacent to public parks and recreation areas;

"(B) provide emergency phone lines to contact law enforcement or security personnel in areas within or adjacent to public parks and recreation areas;

"(C) increase security personnel within or adjacent to public parks and recreation areas; and

"(D) fund any other project intended to increase the security and safety of public parks and recreation areas.

"(2) ELIGIBILITY- In addition to the requirements for project approval imposed by this section, eligibility for assistance under this subsection shall be dependent upon a showing of need. In providing funds under this subsection, the Secretary shall give priority to projects proposed for urban parks and recreation areas with the highest rates of crime and, in particular, to urban parks and recreation areas with the highest rates of sexual assault.

"(3) FEDERAL SHARE- Notwithstanding subsection (c), the Secretary may provide 70 percent improvement grants for projects undertaken by any State for the purposes described in this subsection, and the remaining share of the cost shall be borne by the State.".

CHAPTER 4—NEW EVIDENTIARY RULES

SECTION 40141. SEXUAL HISTORY IN CRIMINAL AND CIVIL CASES.

(a) MODIFICATION OF PROPOSED AMENDMENT- The proposed amendments to the Federal Rules of Evidence that are embraced by an order entered by the Supreme Court of the United States on April 29, 1994, shall take effect on December 1, 1994, as otherwise provided by law, but with the amendment made by subsection (b).

(b) RULE- Rule 412 of the Federal Rules of Evidence is amended to read as follows:

"Rule 412. Sex Offense Cases; Relevance of Alleged Victim's Past Sexual Behavior or Alleged Sexual Predisposition

"(a) EVIDENCE GENERALLY INADMISSIBLE- The following evidence is not admissible in any civil or criminal proceeding involving alleged sexual misconduct except as provided in subdivisions (b) and (c):

"(1) Evidence offered to prove that any alleged victim engaged in other sexual behavior.

"(2) Evidence offered to prove any alleged victim's sexual predisposition.

"(b) EXCEPTIONS-

"(1) In a criminal case, the following evidence is admissible, if otherwise admissible under these rules:

"(A) evidence of specific instances of sexual behavior by the alleged victim offered to prove that a person other than the accused was the source of semen, injury or other physical evidence;

"(B) evidence of specific instances of sexual behavior by the alleged victim with respect to the person accused of the sexual misconduct offered by the accused to prove consent or by the prosecution; and

"(C) evidence the exclusion of which would violate the constitutional rights of the defendant.

"(2) In a civil case, evidence offered to prove the sexual behavior or sexual predisposition of any alleged victim is admissible if it is otherwise admissible under these rules and its probative value substantially outweighs the danger of harm to any victim and of unfair prejudice to any party. Evidence of an alleged victim's reputation is admissible only if it has been placed in controversy by the alleged victim.

"(c) PROCEDURE TO DETERMINE ADMISSIBILITY-

"(1) A party intending to offer evidence under subdivision (b) must—

"(A) file a written motion at least 14 days before trial specifically describing the evidence and stating the purpose for which it is offered unless the court, for good cause requires a different time for filing or permits filing during trial; and

"(B) serve the motion on all parties and notify the alleged victim or, when appropriate, the alleged victim's guardian or representative.

"(2) Before admitting evidence under this rule the court must conduct a hearing in camera and afford the victim and parties a right to attend and be heard. The motion, related papers, and the record of the hearing must be sealed and remain under seal unless the court orders otherwise.".

CHAPTER 5—ASSISTANCE TO VICTIMS OF SEXUAL ASSAULT

SECTION 40151. EDUCATION AND PREVENTION GRANTS TO REDUCE SEXUAL ASSAULTS AGAINST WOMEN.

Part A of title XIX of the Public Health and Human Services Act (42 U.S.C. 300w et seq.) is amended by adding at the end the following new section:

"SECTION 1910A. USE OF ALLOTMENTS FOR RAPE PREVENTION EDUCATION.

"(a) PERMITTED USE- Notwithstanding section 1904(a)(1), amounts transferred by the State for use under this part may be used for rape prevention and education programs conducted by rape crisis centers or similar nongovernmental nonprofit entities for—

"(1) educational seminars;

"(2) the operation of hotlines;

"(3) training programs for professionals;

"(4) the preparation of informational materials; and

"(5) other efforts to increase awareness of the facts about, or to help prevent, sexual assault, including efforts to increase awareness in underserved racial, ethnic, and language minority communities.

"(b) TARGETING OF EDUCATION PROGRAMS- States providing grant monies must ensure that at least 25 percent of the monies are devoted to education programs targeted for middle school, junior high school, and high school students.

"(c) AUTHORIZATION OF APPROPRIATIONS- There are authorized to be appropriated to carry out this section—

"(1) $35,000,000 for fiscal year 1996;

"(2) $35,000,000 for fiscal year 1997;

"(3) $45,000,000 for fiscal year 1998;

"(4) $45,000,000 for fiscal year 1999; and

"(5) $45,000,000 for fiscal year 2000.

"(d) LIMITATION- Funds authorized under this section may only be used for providing rape prevention and education programs.

"(e) DEFINITION- For purposes of this section, the term "rape prevention and education' includes education and prevention efforts directed at offenses committed by offenders who are not known to the victim as well as offenders who are known to the victim.

"(f) TERMS- The Secretary shall make allotments to each State on the basis of the population of the State, and subject to the conditions provided in this section and sections 1904 through 1909.".

SECTION 40152. TRAINING PROGRAMS.

(a) IN GENERAL- The Attorney General, after consultation with victim advocates and individuals who have expertise in treating sex offenders, shall establish criteria and develop training programs to assist probation and parole officers and other personnel who work with released sex offenders in the areas of—

(1) case management;

(2) supervision; and

(3) relapse prevention.

(b) TRAINING PROGRAMS- The Attorney General shall ensure, to the extent practicable, that training programs developed under subsection (a) are available in geographically diverse locations throughout the country.

(c) AUTHORIZATION OF APPROPRIATIONS- There are authorized to be appropriated to carry out this section—

(1) $1,000,000 for fiscal year 1996; and

(2) $1,000,000 for fiscal year 1997.

SECTION 40153. CONFIDENTIALITY OF COMMUNICATIONS BETWEEN SEXUAL ASSAULT OR DOMESTIC VIOLENCE VICTIMS AND THEIR COUNSELORS.

(a) STUDY AND DEVELOPMENT OF MODEL LEGISLATION- The Attorney General shall—

(1) study and evaluate the manner in which the States have taken measures to protect the confidentiality of communications between sexual assault or domestic violence victims and their therapists or trained counselors;

(2) develop model legislation that will provide the maximum protection possible for the confidentiality of such communications, within any applicable constitutional limits, taking into account the following factors:

(A) the danger that counseling programs for victims of sexual assault and domestic violence will be unable to achieve their goal of helping victims recover from the trauma associated with these crimes if there is no assurance that the records of the counseling sessions will be kept confidential;

(B) consideration of the appropriateness of an absolute privilege for communications between victims of sexual assault or domestic violence and their therapists or trained counselors, in light of the likelihood that such an absolute privilege will provide the maximum guarantee of confidentiality but also in light of the possibility that such an absolute privilege may be held to violate the rights of criminal defendants under the Federal or State constitutions by denying them the opportunity to obtain exculpatory evidence and present it at trial; and

(C) consideration of what limitations on the disclosure of confidential communications between victims of these crimes and their counselors, short of an absolute privilege, are most likely to ensure that the counseling programs will not be undermined, and specifically whether no such disclosure should be allowed unless, at a minimum, there has been a particularized showing by a criminal defendant of a compelling need for records of such communications, and adequate procedural safeguards are in place to prevent unnecessary or damaging disclosures; and

(3) prepare and disseminate to State authorities the findings made and model legislation developed as a result of the study and evaluation.

(b) REPORT AND RECOMMENDATIONS- Not later than the date that is 1 year after the date of enactment of this Act, the Attorney General shall report to the Congress—

(1) the findings of the study and the model legislation required by this section; and

(2) recommendations based on the findings on the need for and appropriateness of further action by the Federal Government.

(c) REVIEW OF FEDERAL EVIDENTIARY RULES- The Judicial Conference of the United States shall evaluate and report to Congress its views on whether the Federal Rules of Evidence should be amended, and if so, how they should be amended, to guarantee that the confidentiality of communications between sexual assault victims and their therapists or trained counselors will be adequately protected in Federal court proceedings.

SECTION 40154. INFORMATION PROGRAMS.

The Attorney General shall compile information regarding sex offender treatment programs and ensure that information regarding community treatment programs in the community into which a convicted sex offender is released is made available to each person serving a sentence of imprisonment in a Federal penal or correctional institution for a commission of an offense under chapter 109A of title 18, United States Code, or for the commission of a similar offense, including halfway houses and psychiatric institutions.

APPENDIX 2:

SUBTITLE B—SAFE HOMES FOR WOMEN

SECTION 40201. SHORT TITLE.

This title may be cited as the "Safe Homes for Women Act of 1994".

CHAPTER 1—NATIONAL DOMESTIC VIOLENCE HOTLINE

SECTION 40211. GRANT FOR A NATIONAL DOMESTIC VIOLENCE HOTLINE.

The Family Violence Prevention and Services Act (42 U.S.C. 10401 et seq.) is amended by adding at the end the following new section:

"SECTION 316. NATIONAL DOMESTIC VIOLENCE HOTLINE GRANT.

"(a) IN GENERAL- The Secretary may award a grant to a private, nonprofit entity to provide for the operation of a national, toll-free telephone hotline to provide information and assistance to victims of domestic violence.

"(b) DURATION- A grant under this section may extend over a period of not more than 5 years.

"(c) ANNUAL APPROVAL- The provision of payments under a grant under this section shall be subject to annual approval by the Secretary and subject to the availability of appropriations for each fiscal year to make the payments.

"(d) ACTIVITIES- Funds received by an entity under this section shall be used to establish and operate a national, toll-free telephone hotline to provide information and assistance to victims of domestic violence. In establishing and operating the hotline, a private, non-profit entity shall—

"(1) contract with a carrier for the use of a toll-free telephone line;

"(2) employ, train, and supervise personnel to answer incoming calls and provide counseling and referral services to callers on a 24-hour-a-day basis;

"(3) assemble and maintain a current database of information relating to services for victims of domestic violence to which callers may be referred throughout the United States, including information on the availability of shelters that serve battered women; and

"(4) publicize the hotline to potential users throughout the United States.

"(e) APPLICATION- A grant may not be made under this section unless an application for such grant has been approved by the Secretary. To be approved by the Secretary under this subsection an application shall—

"(1) contain such agreements, assurances, and information, be in such form and be submitted in such manner as the Secretary shall prescribe through notice in the Federal Register;

"(2) include a complete description of the applicant's plan for the operation of a national domestic violence hotline, including descriptions of—

"(A) the training program for hotline personnel;

"(B) the hiring criteria for hotline personnel;

"(C) the methods for the creation, maintenance and updating of a resource database;

"(D) a plan for publicizing the availability of the hotline;

"(E) a plan for providing service to non-English speaking callers, including hotline personnel who speak Spanish; and

"(F) a plan for facilitating access to the hotline by persons with hearing impairments;

"(3) demonstrate that the applicant has nationally recognized expertise in the area of domestic violence and a record of high quality service to victims of domestic violence, including a demonstration of support from advocacy groups, such as domestic violence State coalitions or recognized national domestic violence groups;

"(4) demonstrates that the applicant has a commitment to diversity, and to the provision of services to ethnic, racial, and non-English speaking minorities, in addition to older individuals and individuals with disabilities; and

"(5) contain such other information as the Secretary may require.

"(f) AUTHORIZATION OF APPROPRIATIONS-

"(1) IN GENERAL- There are authorized to be appropriated to carry out this section—

"(A) $1,000,000 for fiscal year 1995;

"(B) $400,000 for fiscal year 1996;

"(C) $400,000 for fiscal year 1997;

"(D) $400,000 for fiscal year 1998;

"(E) $400,000 for fiscal year 1999; and

"(F) $400,000 for fiscal year 2000.

"(2) AVAILABILITY- Funds authorized to be appropriated under paragraph (1) shall remain available until expended.'.

CHAPTER 2—INTERSTATE ENFORCEMENT

SECTION 40221. INTERSTATE ENFORCEMENT.

(a) IN GENERAL- Part 1 of title 18, United States Code, is amended by inserting after chapter 110 the following new chapter:

"CHAPTER 110A—DOMESTIC VIOLENCE

"Section 2261. Interstate domestic violence

"(a) OFFENSES-

"(1) CROSSING A STATE LINE- A person who travels across a State line or enters or leaves Indian country with the intent to injure, harass, or intimidate that person's spouse or intimate partner, and who, in the course of or as a result of such travel, intentionally commits a crime of violence and thereby causes bodily injury to such spouse or intimate partner, shall be punished as provided in subsection (b).

"(2) CAUSING THE CROSSING OF A STATE LINE- A person who causes a spouse or intimate partner to cross a State line or to enter or leave Indian country by force, coercion, duress, or fraud and, in the course or as a result of that conduct, intentionally commits a crime of violence and thereby causes bodily injury to the person's spouse or intimate partner, shall be punished as provided in subsection (b).

"(b) PENALTIES- A person who violates this section shall be fined under this title, imprisoned—

"(1) for life or any term of years, if death of the offender's spouse or intimate partner results;

"(2) for not more than 20 years if permanent disfigurement or life threatening bodily injury to the offender's spouse or intimate partner results;

"(3) for not more than 10 years, if serious bodily injury to the offender's spouse or intimate partner results or if the offender uses a dangerous weapon during the offense;

"(4) as provided for the applicable conduct under chapter 109A if the offense would constitute an offense under chapter 109A (without regard to whether the offense was committed in the special maritime and territorial jurisdiction of the United States or in a Federal prison); and

"(5) for not more than 5 years, in any other case, or both fined and imprisoned.

"Section 2262. Interstate violation of protection order

"(a) OFFENSES-

"(1) CROSSING A STATE LINE- A person who travels across a State line or enters or leaves Indian country with the intent to engage in conduct that—

"(A)(i) violates the portion of a protection order that involves protection against credible threats of violence, repeated harassment, or bodily injury to the person or persons for whom the protection order was issued; or "(ii) would violate subparagraph (A) if the conduct occurred in the jurisdiction in which the order was issued; and

"(B) subsequently engages in such conduct, shall be punished as provided in subsection (b).

"(2) CAUSING THE CROSSING OF A STATE LINE- A person who causes a spouse or intimate partner to cross a State line or to enter or leave Indian country by force, coercion, duress, or fraud, and, in the course or as a result of that conduct, intentionally commits an act that injures the person's spouse or intimate partner in violation of a valid protection order issued by a State shall be punished as provided in subsection (b).

"(b) PENALTIES- A person who violates this section shall be fined under this title, imprisoned—

"(1) for life or any term of years, if death of the offender's spouse or intimate partner results;

"(2) for not more than 20 years if permanent disfigurement or life threatening bodily injury to the offender's spouse or intimate partner results;

"(3) for not more than 10 years, if serious bodily injury to the offender's spouse or intimate partner results or if the offender uses a dangerous weapon during the offense;

"(4) as provided for the applicable conduct under chapter 109A if the offense would constitute an offense under chapter 109A (without regard to whether the offense was committed in the special maritime and territorial jurisdiction of the United States or in a Federal prison); and

"(5) for not more than 5 years, in any other case, or both fined and imprisoned.

"Section 2263. Pretrial release of defendant

"In any proceeding pursuant to section 3142 for the purpose of determining whether a defendant charged under this chapter shall be released pending trial, or for the purpose of determining conditions of such release, the alleged victim shall be given an opportunity to be heard regarding the danger posed by the defendant.

"Section 2264. Restitution

"(a) IN GENERAL- Notwithstanding section 3663, and in addition to any other civil or criminal penalty authorized by law, the court shall order restitution for any offense under this chapter.

"(b) SCOPE AND NATURE OF ORDER-

"(1) DIRECTIONS- The order of restitution under this section shall direct that—

"(A) the defendant pay to the victim (through the appropriate court mechanism) the full amount of the victim's losses as determined by the court, pursuant to paragraph (3); and

"(B) the United States Attorney enforce the restitution order by all available and reasonable means.

"(2) ENFORCEMENT BY VICTIM- An order of restitution also may be enforced by a victim named in the order to receive the restitution in the same manner as a judgment in a civil action.

"(3) DEFINITION- For purposes of this subsection, the term "full amount of the victim's losses' includes any costs incurred by the victim for—

"(A) medical services relating to physical, psychiatric, or psychological care;

"(B) physical and occupational therapy or rehabilitation;

"(C) necessary transportation, temporary housing, and child care expenses;

"(D) lost income;

"(E) attorneys' fees, plus any costs incurred in obtaining a civil protection order; and

"(F) any other losses suffered by the victim as a proximate result of the offense.

"(4) ORDER MANDATORY- (A) The issuance of a restitution order under this section is mandatory.

"(B) A court may not decline to issue an order under this section because of—

"(i) the economic circumstances of the defendant; or

"(ii) the fact that a victim has, or is entitled to, receive compensation for his or her injuries from the proceeds of insurance or any other source.

"(C)(i) Notwithstanding subparagraph (A), the court may take into account the economic circumstances of the defendant in determining the manner in which and the schedule according to which the restitution is to be paid.

"(ii) For purposes of this subparagraph, the term 'economic circumstances' includes—

"(I) the financial resources and other assets of the defendant;

"(II) projected earnings, earning capacity, and other income of the defendant; and

"(III) any financial obligations of the defendant, including obligations to dependents.

"(D) Subparagraph (A) does not apply if—

"(i) the court finds on the record that the economic circumstances of the defendant do not allow for the payment of any amount of a restitution order, and do not allow for the payment of any or some portion of the amount of a restitution order in the foreseeable future (under any reasonable schedule of payments); and

"(ii) the court enters in its order the amount of the victim's losses, and provides a nominal restitution award.

"(5) MORE THAN 1 OFFENDER- When the court finds that more than 1 offender has contributed to the loss of a victim, the court may make each offender liable for payment of the full amount of restitution or may apportion liability among the offenders to reflect the level of contribution and economic circumstances of each offender.

"(6) MORE THAN 1 VICTIM- When the court finds that more than 1 victim has sustained a loss requiring restitution by an offender, the court shall order full restitution of each victim but may provide for different payment schedules to reflect the economic circumstances of each victim.

"(7) PAYMENT SCHEDULE- An order under this section may direct the defendant to make a single lump-sum payment or partial payments at specified intervals.

"(8) SETOFF- Any amount paid to a victim under this section shall be set off against any amount later recovered as compensatory damages by the victim from the defendant in—

"(A) any Federal civil proceeding; and

"(B) any State civil proceeding, to the extent provided by the law of the State.

"(9) EFFECT ON OTHER SOURCES OF COMPENSATION- The issuance of a restitution order shall not affect the entitlement of a victim to receive compensation with respect to a loss from insurance or any other source until the payments actually received by the victim under the restitution order fully compensate the victim for the loss.

"(10) CONDITION OF PROBATION OR SUPERVISED RELEASE- Compliance with a restitution order issued under this section shall be a condition of any probation or supervised release of a defendant. If an offender fails to comply with a restitution order, the court may, after a hearing, revoke probation or a term of supervised release, modify the terms or conditions of probation or a term of supervised release, or hold the defendant in contempt pursuant to section 3583(e). In determining whether to revoke probation or a term of supervised release, modify the terms or conditions of probation or supervised release or hold a defendant serving a term of supervised release in contempt, the court shall consider the defendant's employment status, earning ability and financial resources, the willfulness of the defendant's failure to comply, and any other circumstances that may have a bearing on the defendant's ability to comply.

"(c) AFFIDAVIT- Within 60 days after conviction and, in any event, not later than 10 days before sentencing, the United States Attorney (or such Attorney's delegate), after consulting with the victim, shall prepare and file an affidavit with the court listing the amounts subject to restitution under this section. The affidavit shall be signed by the United States Attorney (or the delegate) and the victim. Should the victim object to any of the information included in the affidavit, the United States Attorney (or the delegate) shall advise the victim that the victim may file a separate affidavit and assist the victim in the preparation of the affidavit.

"(d) OBJECTION- If, after the defendant has been notified of the affidavit, no objection is raised by the defendant, the amounts attested to in the affidavit filed pursuant to subsection (a) shall be entered in the court's restitution order. If objection is raised, the court may require the victim or the United States Attorney (or the United States Attorney's delegate) to submit further affidavits or other supporting documents, demonstrating the victim's losses.

"(e) ADDITIONAL DOCUMENTATION AND TESTIMONY- If the court concludes, after reviewing the supporting documentation and considering the defendant's objections, that there is a substantial reason for doubting the authenticity or veracity of the records submitted, the court may require additional documentation or hear testimony on those questions. The privacy of any records filed, or testimony heard, pursuant to this section, shall be maintained to the greatest extent possible, and such records may be filed or testimony heard in camera.

"(f) FINAL DETERMINATION OF LOSSES- If the victim's losses are not ascertainable 10 days before sentencing as provided in subsection (c), the United States Attorney (or the United States Attorney's delegate) shall so inform the court, and the court shall set a date for the final determination of the victim's losses, not to exceed 90 days after sentencing. If the victim subsequently discovers further losses, the victim shall have 90 days after discovery of those losses in which to petition the court for an amended restitution order. Such order may be granted only upon a showing of good cause for the failure to include such losses in the initial claim for restitutionary relief.

"(g) RESTITUTION IN ADDITION TO PUNISHMENT- An award of restitution to the victim of an offense under this chapter is not a substitute for imposition of punishment under this chapter.

"Sec. 2265. Full faith and credit given to protection orders

"(a) FULL FAITH AND CREDIT- Any protection order issued that is consistent with subsection (b) of this section by the court of one State or Indian tribe (the issuing State or Indian tribe) shall be accorded full faith and credit by the court of another State or Indian tribe (the enforcing State or Indian tribe) and enforced as if it were the order of the enforcing State or tribe.

"(b) PROTECTION ORDER- A protection order issued by a State or tribal court is consistent with this subsection if—

"(1) such court has jurisdiction over the parties and matter under the law of such State or Indian tribe; and

"(2) reasonable notice and opportunity to be heard is given to the person against whom the order is sought sufficient to protect that person's right to due process. In the case of ex parte orders, notice and opportunity to be heard must be provided within the time required by State or tribal law, and in any event within a reasonable time after the order is issued, sufficient to protect the respondent's due process rights.

"(c) CROSS OR COUNTER PETITION- A protection order issued by a State or tribal court against one who has petitioned, filed a complaint, or otherwise filed a written pleading for protection against abuse by a spouse or intimate partner is not entitled to full faith and credit if—

"(1) no cross or counter petition, complaint, or other written pleading was filed seeking such a protection order; or

"(2) a cross or counter petition has been filed and the court did not make specific findings that each party was entitled to such an order.

"Section 2266. Definitions

"In this chapter—

"'Bodily Injury' means any act, except one done in self-defense, that results in physical injury or sexual abuse. 'Indian country' has the meaning stated in section 1151. 'Protection order' includes any injunction or other order issued for the purpose of preventing violent or threatening acts or harassment against, or contact or communication with or physical proximity to, another person, including temporary and final orders issued by civil and criminal courts (other than support or child custody orders) whether obtained by filing an independent action or as a pendente lite order in another proceeding so long as any civil order was issued in response to a complaint, petition or motion filed by or on behalf of a person seeking protection.'spouse or intimate partner' includes—

"(A) a spouse, a former spouse, a person who shares a child in common with the abuser, and a person who cohabits or has cohabited with the abuser as a spouse; and

"(B) any other person similarly situated to a spouse who is protected by the domestic or family violence laws of the State in which the injury occurred or where the victim resides.'State' includes a State of the United States, the District of Columbia, a commonwealth, territory, or possession of the United States.

"'Travel Across State Lines' does not include travel across State lines by an individual who is a member of an Indian tribe when such individual remains at all times in the territory of the Indian tribe of which the individual is a member.".

CHAPTER 3—ARREST POLICIES IN DOMESTIC VIOLENCE CASES

SECTION 40231. ENCOURAGING ARREST POLICIES.

(a) IN GENERAL- Title I of the Omnibus Crime Control and Safe Streets Act of 1968 (42 U.S.C. 3711 et seq.), as amended by section 40121(a), is amended—

(1) by redesignating part U as part V;

(2) by redesignating section 2101 as section 2201; and

(3) by inserting after part T the following new part:

"PART U—GRANTS TO ENCOURAGE ARREST POLICIES

"SECTION 2101. GRANTS.

"(a) PURPOSE- The purpose of this part is to encourage States, Indian tribal governments, and units of local government to treat domestic violence as a serious violation of criminal law.

"(b) GRANT AUTHORITY- The Attorney General may make grants to eligible States, Indian tribal governments, or units of local government for the following purposes:

"(1) To implement mandatory arrest or proarrest programs and policies in police departments, including mandatory arrest programs and policies for protection order violations.

"(2) To develop policies and training in police departments to improve tracking of cases involving domestic violence.

"(3) To centralize and coordinate police enforcement, prosecution, or judicial responsibility for domestic violence cases in groups or units of police officers, prosecutors, or judges.

"(4) To coordinate computer tracking systems to ensure communication between police, prosecutors, and both criminal and family courts.

"(5) To strengthen legal advocacy service programs for victims of domestic violence.

"(6) To educate judges in criminal and other courts about domestic violence and to improve judicial handling of such cases.

"(c) ELIGIBILITY- Eligible grantees are States, Indian tribal governments, or units of local government that—

"(1) certify that their laws or official policies—

"(A) encourage or mandate arrests of domestic violence offenders based on probable cause that an offense has been committed; and

"(B) encourage or mandate arrest of domestic violence offenders who violate the terms of a valid and outstanding protection order;

"(2) demonstrate that their laws, policies, or practices and their training programs discourage dual arrests of offender and victim;

"(3) certify that their laws, policies, or practices prohibit issuance of mutual restraining orders of protection except in cases where both spouses file a claim and the court makes detailed findings of fact indicating that both spouses acted primarily as aggressors and that neither spouse acted primarily in self-defense; and

"(4) certify that their laws, policies, or practices do not require, in connection with the prosecution of any misdemeanor or felony domestic violence offense, that the abused bear the costs associated with the filing of criminal charges or the service of such charges on an abuser, or that the abused bear the costs associated with the issuance or service of a warrant, protection order, or witness subpoena.

"SECTION 2102. APPLICATIONS.

"(a) APPLICATION- An eligible grantee shall submit an application to the Attorney General that—

"(1) contains a certification by the chief executive officer of the State, Indian tribal government, or local government entity that the conditions of section 2101(c) are met or will be met within the later of—

"(A) the period ending on the date on which the next session of the State or Indian tribal legislature ends; or

"(B) 2 years of the date of enactment of this part;

"(2) describes plans to further the purposes stated in section 2101(a);

"(3) identifies the agency or office or groups of agencies or offices responsible for carrying out the program; and

"(4) includes documentation from nonprofit, private sexual assault and domestic violence programs demonstrating their participation in developing the application, and identifying such programs in which such groups will be consulted for development and implementation.

"(b) PRIORITY- In awarding grants under this part, the Attorney General shall give priority to applicants that—

"(1) do not currently provide for centralized handling of cases involving domestic violence by police, prosecutors, and courts; and

"(2) demonstrate a commitment to strong enforcement of laws, and prosecution of cases, involving domestic violence.

"SECTION 2105. DEFINITIONS.

"For purposes of this part—

"(1) the term 'Domestic Violence' includes felony or misdemeanor crimes of violence committed by a current or former spouse of the victim, by a person with whom the victim shares a child in common, by a person who is cohabiting with or has cohabited with the victim as a spouse, by a person similarly situated to a spouse of the victim under the domestic or family violence laws of the jurisdiction receiving grant monies, or by any other adult person against a victim who is protected from that person's acts under the domestic or family violence laws of the eligible State, Indian tribal government, or unit of local government that receives a grant under this part; and

"(2) the term 'Protection Order' includes any injunction issued for the purpose of preventing violent or threatening acts of domestic violence, including temporary and final orders issued by civil or criminal courts (other than support or child custody orders or provisions) whether obtained by filing an independent action or as a pendente lite order in another proceeding.".

"PART V—TRANSITION—EFFECTIVE DATE—REPEALER

"Section 2201. Continuation of rules, authorities, and proceedings.".

(c) AUTHORIZATION OF APPROPRIATIONS- Section 1001(a) of title I of the Omnibus Crime Control and Safe Streets Act of 1968 (42 U.S.C. 3793), as amended by section 40121(c), is amended—

(1) in paragraph (3) by striking 'and T' and inserting 'T, and U'; and

(2) by adding at the end the following new paragraph:

"(19) There are authorized to be appropriated to carry out part U—

"(A) $28,000,000 for fiscal year 1996;

"(B) $33,000,000 for fiscal year 1997; and

"(C) $59,000,000 for fiscal year 1998."

CHAPTER 4—SHELTER GRANTS

Section 40241. GRANTS FOR BATTERED WOMEN'S SHELTERS.

Section 310(a) of the Family Violence Prevention and Services Act (42 U.S.C. 10409(a)) is amended to read as follows:

"(a) IN GENERAL- There are authorized to be appropriated to carry out this title—

"(1) $50,000,000 for fiscal year 1996;

"(2) $60,000,000 for fiscal year 1997;

"(3) $70,000,000 for fiscal year 1998;

"(4) $72,500,000 for fiscal year 1999; and

"(5) $72,500,000 for fiscal year 2000.'.

CHAPTER 5—YOUTH EDUCATION

SECTION 40251. YOUTH EDUCATION AND DOMESTIC VIOLENCE.

The Family Violence Prevention and Services Act (42 U.S.C. 10401 et seq.), as amended by section 40211, is amended by adding at the end the following new section:

"SECTION 317. YOUTH EDUCATION AND DOMESTIC VIOLENCE.

"(a) GENERAL PURPOSE- For purposes of this section, the Secretary may, in consultation with the Secretary of Education, select, implement and evaluate 4 model programs for education of young people about domestic violence and violence among intimate partners.

"(b) NATURE OF PROGRAM- The Secretary shall select, implement and evaluate separate model programs for 4 different audiences: primary schools, middle schools, secondary schools, and institutions of higher education. The model programs shall be selected, implemented, and evaluated in consultation with educational experts, legal and psychological experts on battering, and victim advocate organizations such as battered women's shelters, State coalitions and resource centers.

"(c) REVIEW AND DISSEMINATION- Not later than 2 years after the date of enactment of this section, the Secretary shall transmit the design and evaluation of the model programs, along with a plan and cost estimate for nationwide distribution, to the relevant committees of Congress for review.

"(d) AUTHORIZATION OF APPROPRIATIONS- There are authorized to be appropriated to carry out this section $400,000 for fiscal year 1996.".

CHAPTER 6—COMMUNITY PROGRAMS ON DOMESTIC VIOLENCE

SECTION 40261. ESTABLISHMENT OF COMMUNITY PROGRAMS ON DOMESTIC VIOLENCE.

The Family Violence Prevention and Services Act (42 U.S.C. 10401 et seq.), as amended by section 40251, is amended by adding at the end the following new section:

"SEC. 318. DEMONSTRATION GRANTS FOR COMMUNITY INITIATIVES.

"(a) IN GENERAL- The Secretary shall provide grants to nonprofit private organizations to establish projects in local communities involving many sectors of each community to coordinate intervention and prevention of domestic violence.

"(b) ELIGIBILITY- To be eligible for a grant under this section, an entity—

"(1) shall be a nonprofit organization organized for the purpose of coordinating community projects for the intervention in and prevention of domestic violence; and

"(2) shall include representatives of pertinent sectors of the local community, which may include—

"(A) health care providers;

"(B) the education community;

"(C) the religious community;

"(D) the justice system;

"(E) domestic violence program advocates;

"(F) human service entities such as State child services divisions;

"(G) business and civic leaders; and

"(H) other pertinent sectors.

"(c) APPLICATIONS- An organization that desires to receive a grant under this section shall submit to the Secretary an application, in such form and in such manner as the Secretary shall prescribe through notice in the Federal Register, that—

"(1) demonstrates that the applicant will serve a community leadership function, bringing together opinion leaders from each sector of the community to develop a coordinated community consensus opposing domestic violence;

"(2) demonstrates a community action component to improve and expand current intervention and prevention strategies through increased communication and coordination among all affected sectors;

"(3) includes a complete description of the applicant's plan for the establishment and operation of the community project, including a description of—

"(A) the method for identification and selection of an administrative committee made up of persons knowledgeable in domestic violence to oversee the project, hire staff, assure compliance with the project outline, and secure annual evaluation of the project;

"(B) the method for identification and selection of project staff and a project evaluator;

"(C) the method for identification and selection of a project council consisting of representatives of the community sectors listed in subsection (b)(2);

"(D) the method for identification and selection of a steering committee consisting of representatives of the various community sectors who will chair subcommittees of the project council focusing on each of the sectors; and

"(E) a plan for developing outreach and public education campaigns regarding domestic violence; and

"(4) contains such other information, agreements, and assurances as the Secretary may require.

"(d) TERM- A grant provided under this section may extend over a period of not more than 3 fiscal years.

"(e) CONDITIONS ON PAYMENT- Payments under a grant under this section shall be subject to—

"(1) annual approval by the Secretary; and

"(2) availability of appropriations.

"(f) GEOGRAPHICAL DISPERSION- The Secretary shall award grants under this section to organizations in communities geographically dispersed throughout the country.

"(g) USE OF GRANT MONIES-

"(1) IN GENERAL- A grant made under subsection (a) shall be used to establish and operate a community project to coordinate intervention and prevention of domestic violence.

"(2) REQUIREMENTS- In establishing and operating a project, a nonprofit private organization shall—

"(A) establish protocols to improve and expand domestic violence intervention and prevention strategies among all affected sectors;

"(B) develop action plans to direct responses within each community sector that are in conjunction with development in all other sectors; and

"(C) provide for periodic evaluation of the project with a written report and analysis to assist application of this concept in other communities.

"(h) AUTHORIZATION OF APPROPRIATIONS- There are authorized to be appropriated to carry out this section—

"(1) $4,000,000 for fiscal year 1996; and

"(2) $6,000,000 for fiscal year 1997.

"(i) REGULATIONS- Not later than 60 days after the date of enactment of this section, the Secretary shall publish proposed regulations implementing this section. Not later than 120 days after the date of enactment, the Secretary shall publish final regulations implementing this section.".

CHAPTER 8—CONFIDENTIALITY FOR ABUSED PERSONS

SECTION 40281. CONFIDENTIALITY OF ABUSED PERSON'S ADDRESS.

(a) REGULATIONS- Not later than 90 days after the date of enactment of this Act, the United States Postal Service shall promulgate regulations to secure the confidentiality of domestic violence shelters and abused persons' addresses.

(b) REQUIREMENTS- The regulations under subsection (a) shall require—

(1) in the case of an individual, the presentation to an appropriate postal official of a valid, outstanding protection order; and

(2) in the case of a domestic violence shelter, the presentation to an appropriate postal authority of proof from a State domestic violence coa-

lition that meets the requirements of section 311 of the Family Violence Prevention and Services Act (42 U.S.C. 10410)) verifying that the organization is a domestic violence shelter.

(c) DISCLOSURE FOR CERTAIN PURPOSES- The regulations under subsection (a) shall not prohibit the disclosure of addresses to State or Federal agencies for legitimate law enforcement or other governmental purposes.

(d) EXISTING COMPILATIONS- Compilations of addresses existing at the time at which order is presented to an appropriate postal official shall be excluded from the scope of the regulations under subsection (a).

CHAPTER 9—DATA AND RESEARCH

SECTION 40291. RESEARCH AGENDA.

(a) REQUEST FOR CONTRACT- The Attorney General shall request the National Academy of Sciences, through its National Research Council, to enter into a contract to develop a research agenda to increase the understanding and control of violence against women, including rape and domestic violence. In furtherance of the contract, the National Academy shall convene a panel of nationally recognized experts on violence against women, in the fields of law, medicine, criminal justice, and direct services to victims and experts on domestic violence in diverse, ethnic, social, and language minority communities and the social sciences. In setting the agenda, the Academy shall focus primarily on preventive, educative, social, and legal strategies, including addressing the needs of underserved populations.

(b) DECLINATION OF REQUEST- If the National Academy of Sciences declines to conduct the study and develop a research agenda, it shall recommend a nonprofit private entity that is qualified to conduct such a study. In that case, the Attorney General shall carry out subsection (a) through the nonprofit private entity recommended by the Academy. In either case, whether the study is conducted by the National Academy of Sciences or by the nonprofit group it recommends, the funds for the contract shall be made available from sums appropriated for the conduct of research by the National Institute of Justice.

(c) REPORT- The Attorney General shall ensure that no later than 1 year after the date of enactment of this Act, the study required under subsection (a) is completed and a report describing the findings made is submitted to the Committee on the Judiciary of the Senate and the Committee on the Judiciary of the House of Representatives.

SECTION 40292. STATE DATABASES.

(a) IN GENERAL- The Attorney General shall study and report to the States and to Congress on how the States may collect centralized databases on the incidence of sexual and domestic violence offenses within a State.

(b) CONSULTATION- In conducting its study, the Attorney General shall consult persons expert in the collection of criminal justice data, State statistical administrators, law enforcement personnel, and nonprofit nongovernmental agencies that provide direct services to victims of domestic violence. The final report shall set forth the views of the persons consulted on the recommendations.

(c) REPORT- The Attorney General shall ensure that no later than 1 year after the date of enactment of this Act, the study required under subsection (a) is completed and a report describing the findings made is submitted to the Committees on the Judiciary of the Senate and the House of Representatives.

(d) AUTHORIZATION OF APPROPRIATIONS- There are authorized to be appropriated to carry out this section $200,000 for fiscal year 1996.

SECTION 40293. NUMBER AND COST OF INJURIES.

(a) STUDY- The Secretary of Health and Human Services, acting through the Centers for Disease Control Injury Control Division, shall conduct a study to obtain a national projection of the incidence of injuries resulting from domestic violence, the cost of injuries to health care facilities, and recommend health care strategies for reducing the incidence and cost of such injuries.

(b) AUTHORIZATION OF APPROPRIATIONS- There are authorized to be appropriated to carry out this section—$100,000 for fiscal year 1996.

CHAPTER 10—RURAL DOMESTIC VIOLENCE
AND CHILD ABUSE ENFORCEMENT

SECTION 40295. RURAL DOMESTIC VIOLENCE AND CHILD ABUSE ENFORCEMENT ASSISTANCE.

(a) GRANTS- The Attorney General may make grants to States, Indian tribal governments, and local governments of rural States, and to other public or private entities of rural States—

(1) to implement, expand, and establish cooperative efforts and projects between law enforcement officers, prosecutors, victim advocacy

groups, and other related parties to investigate and prosecute incidents of domestic violence and child abuse;

(2) to provide treatment and counseling to victims of domestic violence and child abuse; and

(3) to work in cooperation with the community to develop education and prevention strategies directed toward such issues.

(b) DEFINITIONS- In this section—

"Indian Tribe" means a tribe, band, pueblo, nation, or other organized group or community of Indians, including an Alaska Native village (as defined in or established under the Alaska Native Claims Settlement Act (43 U.S.C. 1601 et seq.), that is recognized as eligible for the special programs and services provided by the United States to Indians because of their status as Indians.

"Rural State" has the meaning stated in section 1501(b) of title I of the Omnibus Crime Control and Safe Streets Act of 1968 (42 U.S.C. 3796bb(B)).

(c) AUTHORIZATION OF APPROPRIATIONS-

(1) IN GENERAL- There are authorized to be appropriated to carry out this section—

(A) $7,000,000 for fiscal year 1996;

(B) $8,000,000 for fiscal year 1997; and

(C) $15,000,000 for fiscal year 1998.

(2) ADDITIONAL FUNDING- In addition to funds received under a grant under subsection (a), a law enforcement agency may use funds received under a grant under section 103 to accomplish the objectives of this section.

SUBTITLE C—CIVIL RIGHTS FOR WOMEN

SECTION 40301. SHORT TITLE.

This subtitle may be cited as the "Civil Rights Remedies for Gender-Motivated Violence Act".

SECTION 40302. CIVIL RIGHTS.

(a) PURPOSE- Pursuant to the affirmative power of Congress to enact this subtitle under section 5 of the Fourteenth Amendment to the Constitution, as well as under section 8 of Article I of the Constitution, it is the purpose of this subtitle to protect the civil rights of victims of gender motivated violence and to promote public safety, health, and activities affecting interstate commerce by establishing a Federal civil rights cause of action for victims of crimes of violence motivated by gender.

(b) RIGHT TO BE FREE FROM CRIMES OF VIOLENCE- All persons within the United States shall have the right to be free from crimes of violence motivated by gender (as defined in subsection (d)).

(c) CAUSE OF ACTION- A person (including a person who acts under color of any statute, ordinance, regulation, custom, or usage of any State) who commits a crime of violence motivated by gender and thus deprives another of the right declared in subsection (b) shall be liable to the party injured, in an action for the recovery of compensatory and punitive damages, injunctive and declaratory relief, and such other relief as a court may deem appropriate.

(d) DEFINITIONS- For purposes of this section—

(1) the term "Crime of Violence Motivated by Gender" means a crime of violence committed because of gender or on the basis of gender, and due, at least in part, to an animus based on the victim's gender; and

(2) the term "Crime of Violence" means—

(A) an act or series of acts that would constitute a felony against the person or that would constitute a felony against property if the conduct presents a serious risk of physical injury to another, and that would come within the meaning of State or Federal offenses described in section 16 of title 18, United States Code, whether or not those acts have actually resulted in criminal charges, prosecution, or conviction and whether or not those acts were committed in the special maritime, territorial, or prison jurisdiction of the United States; and

(B) includes an act or series of acts that would constitute a felony described in subparagraph (A) but for the relationship between the person who takes such action and the individual against whom such action is taken.

(e) LIMITATION AND PROCEDURES-

(1) LIMITATION- Nothing in this section entitles a person to a cause of action under subsection (c) for random acts of violence unrelated to gender or for acts that cannot be demonstrated, by a preponderance of the evidence, to be motivated by gender (within the meaning of subsection (d)).

(2) NO PRIOR CRIMINAL ACTION- Nothing in this section requires a prior criminal complaint, prosecution, or conviction to establish the elements of a cause of action under subsection (c).

(3) CONCURRENT JURISDICTION- The Federal and State courts shall have concurrent jurisdiction over actions brought pursuant to this subtitle.

(4) SUPPLEMENTAL JURISDICTION- Neither section 1367 of title 28, United States Code, nor subsection (c) of this section shall be construed, by reason of a claim arising under such subsection, to confer on the courts of the United States jurisdiction over any State law claim seeking the establishment of a divorce, alimony, equitable distribution of marital property, or child custody decree.

(5) LIMITATION ON REMOVAL- Section 1445 of title 28, United States Code, is amended by adding at the end the following new subsection:

"(d) A civil action in any State court arising under section 40302 of the Violence Against Women Act of 1994 may not be removed to any district court of the United States.".

SECTION 40303. ATTORNEY'S FEES.

Section 722 of the Revised Statutes (42 U.S.C. 1988) is amended in the last sentence—

(1) by striking "or" after "Public Law 92-318,"; and

(2) by inserting ", or section 40302 of the Violence Against Women Act of 1994," after "1964".

SECTION 40304. SENSE OF THE SENATE CONCERNING PROTECTION OF THE PRIVACY OF RAPE VICTIMS.

It is the sense of the Senate that news media, law enforcement officers, and other persons should exercise restraint and respect a rape victim's privacy by not disclosing the victim's identity to the general public or facilitating such disclosure without the consent of the victim.

APPENDIX 4:

SUBTITLE D—EQUAL JUSTICE FOR WOMEN IN THE COURTS ACT

SECTION 40401. SHORT TITLE.

This subtitle may be cited as the "Equal Justice for Women in the Courts Act of 1994".

CHAPTER 1—EDUCATION AND TRAINING FOR JUDGES AND COURT PERSONNEL IN STATE COURTS

SECTION 40411. GRANTS AUTHORIZED.

The State Justice Institute may award grants for the purpose of developing, testing, presenting, and disseminating model programs to be used by States (as defined in section 202 of the State Justice Institute Act of 1984 (42 U.S.C. 10701)) in training judges and court personnel in the laws of the States and by Indian tribes in training tribal judges and court personnel in the laws of the tribes on rape, sexual assault, domestic violence, and other crimes of violence motivated by the victim's gender.

SECTION 40412. TRAINING PROVIDED BY GRANTS.

Training provided pursuant to grants made under this subtitle may include current information, existing studies, or current data on—

(1) the nature and incidence of rape and sexual assault by strangers and nonstrangers, marital rape, and incest;

(2) the underreporting of rape, sexual assault, and child sexual abuse;

(3) the physical, psychological, and economic impact of rape and sexual assault on the victim, the costs to society, and the implications for sentencing;

(4) the psychology of sex offenders, their high rate of recidivism, and the implications for sentencing;

(5) the historical evolution of laws and attitudes on rape and sexual assault;

(6) sex stereotyping of female and male victims of rape and sexual assault, racial stereotyping of rape victims and defendants, and the impact of such stereotypes on credibility of witnesses, sentencing, and other aspects of the administration of justice;

(7) application of rape shield laws and other limits on introduction of evidence that may subject victims to improper sex stereotyping and harassment in both rape and nonrape cases, including the need for sua sponte judicial intervention in inappropriate cross-examination;

(8) the use of expert witness testimony on rape trauma syndrome, child sexual abuse accommodation syndrome, post-traumatic stress syndrome, and similar issues;

(9) the legitimate reasons why victims of rape, sexual assault, and incest may refuse to testify against a defendant;

(10) the nature and incidence of domestic violence;

(11) the physical, psychological, and economic impact of domestic violence on the victim, the costs to society, and the implications for court procedures and sentencing;

(12) the psychology and self-presentation of batterers and victims and the implications for court proceedings and credibility of witnesses;

(13) sex stereotyping of female and male victims of domestic violence, myths about presence or absence of domestic violence in certain racial, ethnic, religious, or socioeconomic groups, and their impact on the administration of justice;

(14) historical evolution of laws and attitudes on domestic violence;

(15) proper and improper interpretations of the defenses of self-defense and provocation, and the use of expert witness testimony on battered woman syndrome;

(16) the likelihood of retaliation, recidivism, and escalation of violence by batterers, and the potential impact of incarceration and other meaningful sanctions for acts of domestic violence including violations of orders of protection;

(17) economic, psychological, social and institutional reasons for victims' inability to leave the batterer, to report domestic violence or to follow through on complaints, including the influence of lack of support from police, judges, and court personnel, and the legitimate reasons why victims of domestic violence may refuse to testify against a defendant;

(18) the need for orders of protection, and the implications of mutual orders of protection, dual arrest policies, and mediation in domestic violence cases; and

(19) recognition of and response to gender-motivated crimes of violence other than rape, sexual assault and domestic violence, such as mass or serial murder motivated by the gender of the victims.

SECTION 40413. COOPERATION IN DEVELOPING PROGRAMS IN MAKING GRANTS UNDER THIS TITLE.

The State Justice Institute shall ensure that model programs carried out pursuant to grants made under this subtitle are developed with the participation of law enforcement officials, public and private nonprofit victim advocates, legal experts, prosecutors, defense attorneys, and recognized experts on gender bias in the courts.

SECTION 40414. AUTHORIZATION OF APPROPRIATIONS.

(a) IN GENERAL- There are authorized to be appropriated to carry out this chapter $600,000 for fiscal year 1996.

(b) MODEL PROGRAMS- Of amounts appropriated under this section, the State Justice Institute shall expend not less than 40 percent on model programs regarding domestic violence and not less than 40 percent on model programs regarding rape and sexual assault.

CHAPTER 2—EDUCATION AND TRAINING FOR JUDGES AND COURT PERSONNEL IN FEDERAL COURTS

SECTION 40421. AUTHORIZATIONS OF CIRCUIT STUDIES; EDUCATION AND TRAINING GRANTS.

(a) STUDIES- In order to gain a better understanding of the nature and the extent of gender bias in the Federal courts, the circuit judicial councils are encouraged to conduct studies of the instances, if any, of gender bias in their respective circuits and to implement recommended reforms.

(b) MATTERS FOR EXAMINATION- The studies under subsection (a) may include an examination of the effects of gender on—

(1) the treatment of litigants, witnesses, attorneys, jurors, and judges in the courts, including before magistrate and bankruptcy judges;

(2) the interpretation and application of the law, both civil and criminal;

(3) treatment of defendants in criminal cases;

(4) treatment of victims of violent crimes in judicial proceedings;

(5) sentencing;

(6) sentencing alternatives and the nature of supervision of probation and parole;

(7) appointments to committees of the Judicial Conference and the courts;

(8) case management and court sponsored alternative dispute resolution programs;

(9) the selection, retention, promotion, and treatment of employees;

(10) appointment of arbitrators, experts, and special masters;

(11) the admissibility of the victim's past sexual history in civil and criminal cases; and

(12) the aspects of the topics listed in section 40412 that pertain to issues within the jurisdiction of the Federal courts.

(c) CLEARINGHOUSE- The Administrative Office of the United States Courts shall act as a clearinghouse to disseminate any reports and materials issued by the gender bias task forces under subsection (a) and to respond to requests for such reports and materials. The gender bias task forces shall provide the Administrative Office of the Courts of the United States with their reports and related material.

(d) MODEL PROGRAMS- The Federal Judicial Center, in carrying out section 620(b)(3) of title 28, United States Code, may—

(1) include in the educational programs it presents and prepares, including the training programs for newly appointed judges, information on issues related to gender bias in the courts including such areas as are listed in subsection (a) along with such other topics as the Federal Judicial Center deems appropriate;

(2) prepare materials necessary to implement this subsection; and

(3) take into consideration the findings and recommendations of the studies conducted pursuant to subsection (a), and to consult with individuals and groups with relevant expertise in gender bias issues as it prepares or revises such materials.

SECTION 40422. AUTHORIZATION OF APPROPRIATIONS.

There are authorized to be appropriated—

(1) to the Salaries and Expenses Account of the Courts of Appeals, District Courts, and other Judicial Services to carry out section 40421(a) $500,000 for fiscal year 1996;

(2) to the Federal Judicial Center to carry out section 40421(d) $100,000 for fiscal year 1996; and

(3) to the Administrative Office of the United States Courts to carry out section 40421(c) $100,000 for fiscal year 1996.

APPENDIX 5:

SUBTITLE E—VIOLENCE AGAINST WOMEN ACT IMPROVEMENTS

SECTION 40501. PRE-TRIAL DETENTION IN SEX OFFENSE CASES.

Section 3156(a)(4) of title 18, United States Code, is amended—

(1) by striking "or" at the end of subparagraph (A);

(2) by striking the period at the end of subparagraph (B) and inserting"; or"; and

(3) by adding after subparagraph (B) the following new subparagraph:

"(C) any felony under chapter 109A or chapter 110.".

SECTION 40502. INCREASED PENALTIES FOR SEX OFFENSES AGAINST VICTIMS BELOW THE AGE OF 16.

Section 2245(2) of title 18, United States Code, is amended—

(1) by striking "or" at the end of subparagraph (B);

(2) by striking "; and" at the end of subparagraph (C) and inserting "; or"; and

(3) by inserting after subparagraph (C) the following new subparagraph:

"(D) the intentional touching, not through the clothing, of the genitalia of another person who has not attained the age of 16 years with an intent to abuse, humiliate, harass, degrade, or arouse or gratify the sexual desire of any person;".

SECTION 40503. PAYMENT OF COST OF TESTING FOR SEXUALLY TRANSMITTED DISEASES.

(a) FOR VICTIMS IN SEX OFFENSE CASES - Section 503(c)(7) of the Victims" Rights and Restitution Act of 1990 (42 U.S.C. 10607(c)(7)) is amended by adding at the end the following: "The Attorney General shall provide for the payment of the cost of up to 2 anonymous and confidential tests of the victim for sexually transmitted diseases, including HIV, gonorrhea, herpes, chlamydia, and syphilis, during the 12 months following sexual assaults that pose a risk of transmission, and the cost of a counseling session by a medically trained professional on the accuracy of such tests and the risk of transmission of sexually transmitted diseases to the victim as the result of the assault. A victim may waive anonymity and confidentiality of any tests paid for under this section.".

(b) Limited Testing of Defendants-

(1) COURT ORDER- The victim of an offense of the type referred to in subsection (a) may obtain an order in the district court of the United States for the district in which charges are brought against the defendant charged with the offense, after notice to the defendant and an opportunity to be heard, requiring that the defendant be tested for the presence of the etiologic agent for acquired immune deficiency syndrome, and that the results of the test be communicated to the victim and the defendant. Any test result of the defendant given to the victim or the defendant must be accompanied by appropriate counseling.

(2) SHOWING REQUIRED- To obtain an order under paragraph (1), the victim must demonstrate that—

(A) the defendant has been charged with the offense in a State or Federal court, and if the defendant has been arrested without a warrant, a probable cause determination has been made;

(B) the test for the etiologic agent for acquired immune deficiency syndrome is requested by the victim after appropriate counseling; and

(C) the test would provide information necessary for the health of the victim of the alleged offense and the court determines that the alleged conduct of the defendant created a risk of transmission, as determined by the Centers for Disease Control, of the etiologic agent for acquired immune deficiency syndrome to the victim.

(3) FOLLOW-UP TESTING- The court may order follow-up tests and counseling under paragraph (b)(1) if the initial test was negative. Such follow-up tests and counseling shall be performed at the request of the victim on dates that occur six months and twelve months following the initial test.

(4) TERMINATION OF TESTING REQUIREMENTS- An order for follow-up testing under paragraph (3) shall be terminated if the person obtains an acquittal on, or dismissal of, all charges of the type referred to in subsection (a).

(5) CONFIDENTIALITY OF TEST- The results of any test ordered under this subsection shall be disclosed only to the victim or, where the court deems appropriate, to the parent or legal guardian of the victim,

and to the person tested. The victim may disclose the test results only to any medical professional, counselor, family member or sexual partner(s) the victim may have had since the attack. Any such individual to whom the test results are disclosed by the victim shall maintain the confidentiality of such information.

(6) DISCLOSURE OF TEST RESULTS- The court shall issue an order to prohibit the disclosure by the victim of the results of any test performed under this subsection to anyone other than those mentioned in paragraph (5). The contents of the court proceedings and test results pursuant to this section shall be sealed. The results of such test performed on the defendant under this section shall not be used as evidence in any criminal trial.

(7) CONTEMPT FOR DISCLOSURE- Any person who discloses the results of a test in violation of this subsection may be held in contempt of court.

(c) PENALTIES FOR INTENTIONAL TRANSMISSION OF HIV- Not later than 6 months after the date of enactment of this Act, the United States Sentencing Commission shall conduct a study and prepare and submit to the committees on the Judiciary of the Senate and the House of Representatives a report concerning recommendations for the revision of sentencing guidelines that relate to offenses in which an HIV infected individual engages in sexual activity if the individual knows that he or she is infected with HIV and intends, through such sexual activity, to expose another to HIV.

SECTION 40504. EXTENSION AND STRENGTHENING OF RESTITUTION.

Section 3663(b) of title 18, United States Code, is amended—

(1) in paragraph (2) by inserting "including an offense under chapter 109A or chapter 110" after "an offense resulting in bodily injury to a victim";

(2) by striking "and" at the end of paragraph (3);

(3) by redesignating paragraph (4) as paragraph (5); and

(4) by inserting after paragraph (3) the following new paragraph:

"(4) in any case, reimburse the victim for lost income and necessary child care, transportation, and other expenses related to participation in the investigation or prosecution of the offense or attendance at proceedings related to the offense; and".

SECTION 40505. ENFORCEMENT OF RESTITUTION ORDERS THROUGH SUSPENSION OF FEDERAL BENEFITS.

Section 3663 of title 18, United States Code, is amended by adding at the end the following new subsection:

"(i)(1) A Federal agency shall immediately suspend all Federal benefits provided by the agency to the defendant, and shall terminate the defendant"s eligibility for Federal benefits administered by that agency, upon receipt of a certified copy of a written judicial finding that the defendant is delinquent in making restitution in accordance with any schedule of payments or any requirement of immediate payment imposed under this section.

"(2) Any written finding of delinquency described in paragraph (1) shall be made by a court, after a hearing, upon motion of the victim named in the order to receive the restitution or upon motion of the United States.

"(3) A defendant found to be delinquent may subsequently seek a written finding from the court that the defendant has rectified the delinquency or that the defendant has made and will make good faith efforts to rectify the delinquency. The defendant"s eligibility for Federal benefits shall be reinstated upon receipt by the agency of a certified copy of such a finding.

"(4) In this subsection, "Federal benefit" means a grant, contract, loan, professional license, or commercial license provided by an agency of the United States.".

SECTION 40506. NATIONAL BASELINE STUDY ON CAMPUS SEXUAL ASSAULT.

(a) STUDY- The Attorney General, in consultation with the Secretary of Education, shall provide for a national baseline study to examine the scope of the problem of campus sexual assaults and the effectiveness of institutional and legal policies in addressing such crimes and protecting victims. The Attorney General may utilize the Bureau of Justice Statistics, the National Institute of Justice, and the Office for Victims of Crime in carrying out this section.

(b) REPORT- Based on the study required by subsection (a) and data collected under the Student Right-To-Know and Campus Security Act (20 U.S.C. 1001 note; Public Law 101-542) and amendments made by that Act, the Attorney General shall prepare a report including an analysis of—

(1) the number of reported allegations and estimated number of unreported allegations of campus sexual assaults, and to whom the allegations are reported (including authorities of the educational institution, sexual assault victim service entities, and local criminal authorities);

(2) the number of campus sexual assault allegations reported to authorities of educational institutions which are reported to criminal authorities;

(3) the number of campus sexual assault allegations that result in criminal prosecution in comparison with the number of non-campus sexual assault allegations that result in criminal prosecution;

(4) Federal and State laws or regulations pertaining specifically to campus sexual assaults;

(5) the adequacy of policies and practices of educational institutions in addressing campus sexual assaults and protecting victims, including consideration of—

(A) the security measures in effect at educational institutions, such as utilization of campus police and security guards, control over access to grounds and buildings, supervision of student activities and student living arrangements, control over the consumption of alcohol by students, lighting, and the availability of escort services;

(B) the articulation and communication to students of the institution's policies concerning sexual assaults;

(C) policies and practices that may prevent or discourage the reporting of campus sexual assaults to local criminal authorities, or that may otherwise obstruct justice or interfere with the prosecution of perpetrators of campus sexual assaults;

(D) the nature and availability of victim services for victims of campus sexual assaults;

(E) the ability of educational institutions" disciplinary processes to address allegations of sexual assault adequately and fairly;

(F) measures that are taken to ensure that victims are free of unwanted contact with alleged assailants, and disciplinary sanctions that are imposed when a sexual assault is determined to have occurred; and

(G) the grounds on which educational institutions are subject to lawsuits based on campus sexual assaults, the resolution of these cases, and measures that can be taken to avoid the likelihood of lawsuits and civil liability;

(6) in conjunction with the report produced by the Department of Education in coordination with institutions of education under the Student Right-To-Know and Campus Security Act (20 U.S.C. 1001 note; Public Law 101-542) and amendments made by that Act, an assessment of the policies and practices of educational institutions that are of greatest effectiveness in addressing campus sexual assaults and protecting victims, including policies and practices relating to the particular issues described in paragraph (5); and

(7) any recommendations the Attorney General may have for reforms to address campus sexual assaults and protect victims more effectively, and any other matters that the Attorney General deems relevant to the subject of the study and report required by this section.

(c) SUBMISSION OF REPORT- The report required by subsection (b) shall be submitted to the Congress no later than September 1, 1996.

(d) DEFINITION- For purposes of this section, "Campus Sexual Assaults" includes sexual assaults occurring at institutions of postsecondary education and sexual assaults committed against or by students or employees of such institutions.

(e) AUTHORIZATION OF APPROPRIATIONS- There are authorized to be appropriated to carry out the study required by this section—$200,000 for fiscal year 1996.

SECTION 40507. REPORT ON BATTERED WOMEN"S SYNDROME.

(a) REPORT- Not less than 1 year after the date of enactment of this Act, the Attorney General and the Secretary of Health and Human Services shall transmit to the House Committee on Energy and Commerce, the Senate Committee on Labor and Human Resources, and the Committees on the Judiciary of the Senate and the House of Representatives a report on the medical and psychological basis of "battered women"s syndrome" and on the extent to which evidence of the syndrome has been considered in criminal trials.

(b) COMPONENTS- The report under subsection (a) shall include—

(1) medical and psychological testimony on the validity of battered women"s syndrome as a psychological condition;

(2) a compilation of State, tribal, and Federal court cases in which evidence of battered women"s syndrome was offered in criminal trials; and

(3) an assessment by State, tribal, and Federal judges, prosecutors, and defense attorneys of the effects that evidence of battered women"s syndrome may have in criminal trials.

SECTION 40508. REPORT ON CONFIDENTIALITY OF ADDRESSES FOR VICTIMS OF DOMESTIC VIOLENCE.

(a) REPORT- The Attorney General shall conduct a study of the means by which abusive spouses may obtain information concerning the addresses or locations of estranged or former spouses, notwithstanding the desire of the victims to have such information withheld to avoid further exposure to abuse. Based on the study, the Attorney General shall transmit a report to Congress including—

(1) the findings of the study concerning the means by which information concerning the addresses or locations of abused spouses may be obtained by abusers; and

(2) analysis of the feasibility of creating effective means of protecting the confidentiality of information concerning the addresses and locations of abused spouses to protect such persons from exposure to further abuse while preserving access to such information for legitimate purposes.

(b) USE OF COMPONENTS- The Attorney General may use the National Institute of Justice and the Office for Victims of Crime in carrying out this section.

SECTION 40509. REPORT ON RECORDKEEPING RELATING TO DOMESTIC VIOLENCE.

Not later than 1 year after the date of enactment of this Act, the Attorney General shall complete a study of, and shall submit to Congress a report and recommendations on, problems of recordkeeping of criminal complaints involving domestic violence. The study and report shall examine—

(1) the efforts that have been made by the Department of Justice, including the Federal Bureau of Investigation, to collect statistics on domestic violence; and

(2) the feasibility of requiring that the relationship between an offender and victim be reported in Federal records of crimes of aggravated assault, rape, and other violent crimes.

APPENDIX 6:

SUBTITLE F—NATIONAL STALKER AND DOMESTIC VIOLENCE REDUCTION

SECTION 40601. AUTHORIZING ACCESS TO FEDERAL CRIMINAL INFORMATION DATABASES.

(a) ACCESS AND ENTRY- Section 534 of title 28, United States Code, is amended by adding at the end the following:

"(e)(1) Information from national crime information databases consisting of identification records, criminal history records, protection orders, and wanted person records may be disseminated to civil or criminal courts for use in domestic violence or stalking cases. Nothing in this subsection shall be construed to permit access to such records for any other purpose.

"(2) Federal and State criminal justice agencies authorized to enter information into criminal information databases may include—

"(A) arrests, convictions, and arrest warrants for stalking or domestic violence or for violations of protection orders for the protection of parties from stalking or domestic violence; and

"(B) protection orders for the protection of persons from stalking or domestic violence, provided such orders are subject to periodic verification.

"(3) As used in this subsection—

"(A) the term "National Crime Information Databases" means the National Crime Information Center and its incorporated criminal history databases, including the Interstate Identification Index; and

"(B) the term "Protection Order" includes an injunction or any other order issued for the purpose of preventing violent or threatening acts or harassment against, or contact or communication with or physical proximity to, another person, including temporary and final orders issued by civil or criminal courts (other than support or child custody orders) whether obtained by filing an independent action or as a pendente lite order in another proceeding so long as any civil order was issued in response to a complaint, petition, or motion filed by or on behalf of a person seeking protection.".

(b) RULEMAKING- The Attorney General may make rules to carry out the subsection added to section 534 of title 28, United States Code, by subsection (a), after consultation with the officials charged with managing the National Crime Information Center and the Criminal Justice Information Services Advisory Policy Board.

SECTION 40602. GRANT PROGRAM.

(a) IN GENERAL- The Attorney General is authorized to provide grants to States and units of local government to improve processes for entering data regarding stalking and domestic violence into local, State, and national crime information databases.

(b) ELIGIBILITY- To be eligible to receive a grant under subsection (a), a State or unit of local government shall certify that it has or intends to establish a program that enters into the National Crime Information Center records of—

(1) warrants for the arrest of persons violating protection orders intended to protect victims from stalking or domestic violence;

(2) arrests or convictions of persons violating protection or domestic violence; and

(3) protection orders for the protection of persons from stalking or domestic violence.

SECTION 40603. AUTHORIZATION OF APPROPRIATIONS.

There are authorized to be appropriated to carry out this subtitle—

(1) $1,500,000 for fiscal year 1996;

(2) $1,750,000 for fiscal year 1997; and

(3) $2,750,000 for fiscal year 1998.

SECTION 40604. APPLICATION REQUIREMENTS.

An application for a grant under this subtitle shall be submitted in such form and manner, and contain such information, as the Attorney General may prescribe. In addition, applications shall include documentation showing—

(1) the need for grant funds and that State or local funding, as the case may be, does not already cover these operations;

(2) intended use of the grant funds, including a plan of action to increase record input; and

(3) an estimate of expected results from the use of the grant funds.

SECTION 40605. DISBURSEMENT.

Not later than 90 days after the receipt of an application under this subtitle, the Attorney General shall either provide grant funds or shall inform the applicant why grant funds are not being provided.

SECTION 40606. TECHNICAL ASSISTANCE, TRAINING, AND EVALUATIONS.

The Attorney General may provide technical assistance and training in furtherance of the purposes of this subtitle, and may provide for the evaluation of programs that receive funds under this subtitle, in addition to any evaluation requirements that the Attorney General may prescribe for grantees. The technical assistance, training, and evaluations authorized by this section may be carried out directly by the Attorney General, or through contracts or other arrangements with other entities.

SECTION 40607. TRAINING PROGRAMS FOR JUDGES.

The State Justice Institute, after consultation with nationally recognized nonprofit organizations with expertise in stalking and domestic violence cases, shall conduct training programs for State (as defined in section 202 of the State Justice Institute Authorization Act of 1984 (42 U.S.C. 10701)) and Indian tribal judges to ensure that a judge issuing an order in a stalking or domestic violence case has all available criminal history and other information, whether from State or Federal sources.

SECTION 40608. RECOMMENDATIONS ON INTRASTATE COMMUNICATION.

The State Justice Institute, after consultation with nationally recognized nonprofit associations with expertise in data sharing among criminal justice agencies and familiarity with the issues raised in stalking and domestic violence cases, shall recommend proposals regarding how State courts may increase intrastate communication between civil and criminal courts.

SECTION 40609. INCLUSION IN NATIONALINCIDENT-BASED REPORTING SYSTEM.

Not later than 2 years after the date of enactment of this Act, the Attorney General, in accordance with the States, shall compile data regarding domes-

tic violence and intimidation (including stalking) as part of the National In-
cident-Based Reporting System (NIBRS).

SECTION 40610. REPORT TO CONGRESS.

The Attorney General shall submit to the Congress an annual report, beginning one year after the date of the enactment of this Act, that provides information concerning the incidence of stalking and domestic violence, and
evaluates the effectiveness of State antistalking efforts and legislation.

SECTION 40611. DEFINITIONS.

As used in this subtitle—

(1) the term "National Crime Information Databases" refers to the
National Crime Information Center and its incorporated criminal history
databases, including the Interstate Identification Index; and

(2) the term "Protection Order" includes an injunction or any other order issued for the purpose of preventing violent or threatening acts or
harassment against, or contact or communication with or physical proximity to, another person, including temporary and final orders issued by
civil or criminal courts (other than support or child custody orders)
whether obtained by filing an independent action or as a pendente lite order in another proceeding so long as any civil order was issued in response to a complaint, petition, or motion filed by or on behalf of a
person seeking protection.

APPENDIX 7:

SUBTITLE G—PROTECTIONS FOR BATTERED IMMIGRANT WOMEN AND CHILDREN

SECTION 40701. ALIEN PETITIONING RIGHTS FOR IMMEDIATE RELATIVE OR SECOND PREFERENCE STATUS.

(a) IN GENERAL- Section 204(a)(1) of the Immigration and Nationality Act (8 U.S.C. 1154(a)(1)) is amended—

(1) in subparagraph (A)—

(A) by inserting "(i)" after "(A)",

(B) by redesignating the second sentence as clause (ii), and

(C) by adding at the end the following new clauses:

"(iii) An alien who is the spouse of a citizen of the United States, who is a person of good moral character, who is eligible to be classified as an immediate relative under section 201(b)(2)(A)(i), and who has resided in the United States with the alien"s spouse may file a petition with the Attorney General under this subparagraph for classification of the alien (and any child of the alien if such a child has not been classified under clause (iv)) under such section if the alien demonstrates to the Attorney General that—

"(I) the alien is residing in the United States, the marriage between the alien and the spouse was entered into in good faith by the alien, and during the marriage the alien or a child of the alien has been battered by or has been the subject of extreme cruelty perpetrated by the alien"s spouse; and

"(II) the alien is a person whose deportation, in the opinion of the Attorney General, would result in extreme hardship to the alien or a child of the alien.

"(iv) An alien who is the child of a citizen of the United States, who is a person of good moral character, who is eligible to be classified as an immediate relative under section 201(b)(2)(A)(i), and who has resided in the United States with the citizen parent may file a petition with the Attorney General under this subparagraph for classification of the alien under such section if the alien demonstrates to the Attorney General that—

"(I) the alien is residing in the United States and during the period of residence with the citizen parent the alien has been battered by or has been the subject of extreme cruelty perpetrated by the alien"s citizen parent; and

"(II) the alien is a person whose deportation, in the opinion of the Attorney General, would result in extreme hardship to the alien.";

(2) in subparagraph (B)—

(A) by inserting "(i)" after "(B)"; and

(B) by adding at the end the following new clauses:

"(ii) An alien who is the spouse of an alien lawfully admitted for permanent residence, who is a person of good moral character, who is eligible for classification under section 203(a)(2)(A), and who has resided in the United States with the alien"s legal permanent resident spouse may file a petition with the Attorney General under this subparagraph for classification of the alien (and any child of the alien if such a child has not been classified under clause (iii)) under such section if the alien demonstrates to the Attorney General that the conditions described in subclauses (I) and (II) of subparagraph (A)(iii) are met with respect to the alien.

"(iii) An alien who is the child of an alien lawfully admitted for permanent residence, who is a person of good moral character, who is eligible for classification under section 203(a)(2)(A), and who has resided in the United States with the alien"s permanent resident alien parent may file a petition with the Attorney General under this subparagraph for classification of the alien under such section if the alien demonstrates to the Attorney General that—

"(I) the alien is residing in the United States and during the period of residence with the permanent resident parent the alien has been battered by or has been the subject of extreme cruelty perpetrated by the alien"s permanent resident parent; and

"(II) the alien is a person whose deportation, in the opinion of the Attorney General, would result in extreme hardship to the alien."; and

(3) by adding at the end the following new subparagraph:

"(H) In acting on petitions filed under clause (iii) or (iv) of subparagraph (A) or clause (ii) or (iii) of subparagraph (B), the Attorney General shall consider any credible evidence relevant to the petition. The determination of what evidence is credible and the weight to be given that evidence shall be within the sole discretion of the Attorney General.".

(b) CONFORMING AMENDMENTS-

(1) Section 204(a)(2) of the Immigration and Nationality Act (8 U.S.C. 1154(a)(2)) is amended—

(A) in subparagraph (A) by striking "filed by an alien who," and inserting "for the classification of the spouse of an alien if the alien,"; and

(B) in subparagraph (B) by striking "by an alien whose prior marriage" and inserting "for the classification of the spouse of an alien if the prior marriage of the alien".

(2) Section 201(b)(2)(A)(i) of the Immigration and Nationality Act (8 U.S.C. 1151(b)(2)(A)(i)) is amended by striking "204(a)(1)(A)" and inserting "204(a)(1)(A)(ii)".

(c) SURVIVAL RIGHTS TO PETITION- Section 204 of the Immigration and Nationality Act (8 U.S.C. 1154) is amended by adding at the end the following new subsection:

"(h) The legal termination of a marriage may not be the sole basis for revocation under section 205 of a petition filed under subsection (a)(1)(A)(iii) or a petition filed under subsection (a)(1)(B)(ii) pursuant to conditions described in subsection (a)(1)(A)(iii)(I).".

(d) EFFECTIVE DATE- The amendments made by this section shall take effect January 1, 1995.

SECTION 40702. USE OF CREDIBLE EVIDENCE IN SPOUSAL WAIVER APPLICATIONS.

(a) IN GENERAL- Section 216(c)(4) of the Immigration and Nationality Act (8 U.S.C. 1186a(c)(4)) is amended by inserting after the second sentence the following: "In acting on applications under this paragraph, the Attorney General shall consider any credible evidence relevant to the application. The determination of what evidence is credible and the weight to be given that evidence shall be within the sole discretion of the Attorney General.".

(b) EFFECTIVE DATE - The amendment made by subsection (a) shall take effect on the date of enactment of this Act and shall apply to applications made before, on, or after such date.

SECTION 40703. SUSPENSION OF DEPORTATION.

(a) BATTERED SPOUSE OR CHILD - Section 244(a) of the Immigration and Nationality Act (8 U.S.C. 1254 (a)) is amended—

(1) by striking "or" at the end of paragraph (1);

(2) by striking the period at the end of paragraph (2) and inserting "; or"; and

(3) by inserting after paragraph (2) the following:

"(3) is deportable under any law of the United States except section 241(a)(1)(G) and the provisions specified in paragraph (2); has been physically present in the United States for a continuous period of not less than 3 years immediately preceding the date of such application; has been battered or subjected to extreme cruelty in the United States by a spouse or parent who is a United States citizen or lawful permanent resident (or is the parent of a child of a United States citizen or lawful permanent resident and the child has been battered or subjected to extreme cruelty in the United States by such citizen or permanent resident parent); and proves that during all of such time in the United States the alien was and is a person of good moral character; and is a person whose deportation would, in the opinion of the Attorney General, result in extreme hardship to the alien or the alien"s parent or child.".

(b) CONSIDERATION OF EVIDENCE- Section 244 of the Immigration and Nationality Act (8 U.S.C. 1254) is amended by adding at the end the following new subsection:

"(g) In acting on applications under subsection (a)(3), the Attorney General shall consider any credible evidence relevant to the application. The determination of what evidence is credible and the weight to be given that evidence shall be within the sole discretion of the Attorney General.".

APPENDIX 8:

TABLE OF TRENDS IN THE NUMBER AND RATES OF
HOMICIDE VICTIMS BY RELATIONSHIP
TO THE OFFENDER (1977 - 1992)

YEAR	WIFE OR GIRLFRIEND	HUSBAND OR BOYFRIEND	OTHER RELATIVE	OTHER KNOWN	STRANGER	UNKNOWN
1977	1396	1185	1683	7113	2562	5162
1978	1428	1095	1701	6199	2640	5886
1979	1438	1137	1674	6909	2682	7574
1980	1498	1129	1797	7304	3064	8248
1981	1486	1149	1869	7837	3491	6666
1982	1408	1008	1807	7290	3551	5904
1983	1487	1043	1796	6681	2897	5445
1984	1420	897	1701	6542	3289	4822
1985	1480	835	1708	7099	2752	5106
1986	1525	866	1690	7708	2679	6142
1987	1508	824	1729	7377	2653	5950
1988	1592	765	1613	7383	2564	6783
1989	1441	817	1741	7568	2817	7117
1990	1524	797	1688	7946	3375	8134
1991	1528	714	1703	7567	3716	9472
1992	1510	657	1531	7550	3218	9295

Source: FBI, Crime in the U.S., 1977-1992.

APPENDIX 9:

DIRECTORY OF NATIONAL DOMESTIC VIOLENCE
ORGANIZATIONS

NAME	ADDRESS	TELEPHONE	FAX
Family Violence Prevention Fund	383 Rhode Island Street, Suite 304, San Francisco, CA 94103-5133	415-252-8900	415-252-8991
Health Resource Center on Domestic Violence	383 Rhode Island Street, Suite 304, San Francisco, CA 94103-5133	800-313-1310	415-252-8991
National Clearinghouse on Marital and Date Rape	2325 Oak Street, Berkeley, CA 94708	510-524-1582	n/a
National Coalition Against Domestic Violence	P.O. Box 18749, Denver, CO 80218	303-839-1852	303-831-9251
National Coalition Against Domestic Violence Policy Office	119 Constitution Avenue NE, Washington, DC 20002	202-544-7358	202-544-7893
National Network to End Domestic Violence	701 Pennsylvania Avenue NW, Suite 900, Washington, DC 20004	202-347-9520	202-434-7400
Battered Women's Justice Project	4032 Chicago Avenue South, Minneapolis, MN 55407	612-824-8768	612-824-8965
Resource Center on Child Custody and Child Protection	P.O. Box 8970, Reno, NV 89507	800-527-3223	702-784-6160
National Resource Center on Domestic Violence	6400 Flank Drive, Suite 1300, Harrisburg, PA 17112	800-537-2238	717-671-8149
National Clearinghouse for the Defense of Battered Women	125 South 9th Street, Suite 302, Philadelphia, PA 19107	800-903- 0111	215-351-0779
Battered Women's Justice Project	524 McKnight Street, Reading, PA 19601	800-903-0111	610-373-6403
National Network to End Domestic Violence	8701 North Mopac Expressway, Suite 450, Austin, TX 78759	512-794-1133	512-794-1199
Center for the Prevention of Sexual and Domestic Violence	936 North 34th Street, Suite 200, Seattle, WA 98103	206-634-1903	206-634-0115

APPENDIX 10:

DIRECTORY OF STATE DOMESTIC
VIOLENCE COALITIONS

STATE	DEPARTMENT	ADDRESS	TELEPHONE	FAX
ALABAMA	Alabama Coalition Against Domestic Violence	P.O. Box 4762, Montgomery, AL 36101	334-832-4842	334-832-4803
ALASKA	Alaska Network on Domestic Violence and Sexual Assault	130 Seward Street, Room 501, Juneau, AK 99801	907-586-3650	907-463-4493
ARIZONA	Arizona Coalition Against Domestic Violence	100 West Camelback Street, Suite 109, Phoenix, AZ 85013	602-279-2900	602-279-2980
ARKANSAS	Arkansas Coalition Against Domestic Violence	#1 Sheriff Lane, Suite C, Little Rock, AR 72114	501-812-0571	501-812-0578
CALIFORNIA	California Alliance Against Domestic Violence	926 J Street, Suite 1000, Sacramento, CA 95814	916-444-7163	916-444-7165
COLORADO	Colorado Domestic Violence Coalition	P.O. Box 18902 Denver, CO 80218	303-831-9632	303-832-7067
CONNECTICUT	Connecticut Coalition Against Domestic Violence	135 Broad Street, Hartford, CT 06105	860-524-5890	860-249-1408
DISTRICT OF COLUMBIA	D.C. Coalition Against Domestic Violence	P.O. Box 76069, Washington, DC 20013	202-783-5332	202-387-5684
DELAWARE	Delaware Coalition Against Domestic Violence	P.O. Box 847, Wilmington, DE 19899	302-658-2958	302-658-5049
GEORGIA	Georgia Advocates for Battered Women and Children	250 Georgia Avenue SE, Suite 308, Atlanta, GA 30312	404-524-3847	404-524-5959
HAWAII	Hawaii State Coalition Against Domestic Violence	98- 939 Moanalua Road, Aiea, HI 96701-5012	808-486-5072	808-486-5169

STATE	DEPARTMENT	ADDRESS	TELEPHONE	FAX
IDAHO	Idaho Coalition Against Sexual and Domestic Violence	815 Park Blvd., Suite 140, Boise, ID 83712	208-384-0419	208-331-0687
ILLINOIS	Illinois Coalition Against Domestic Violence	730 East Vine Street, Suite 109, Springfield, Illinios 62703	217-789-2830	217-789-1939
INDIANA	Indiana Coalition Against Domestic Violence	2511 E. 46th Street, Suite N-3, Indianapolis, IN 46205	317-543-3908	317-568-4045
IOWA	Iowa Coalition Against Domestic Violence	2603 Bell Avenue, Suite 100, Des Moines, IA 50321	515-244-8028	515-244-7417
KANSAS	Kansas Coalition Against Sexual and Domestic Violence	820 SE Quincy, Suite 422, Topeka, KS 66612	785-232-9784	785-232-9937
KENTUCKY	Kentucky Domestic Violence Association	P.O. Box 356, Frankfort, KY 40602	502-875-4132	502-875-4268
LOUISIANA	Louisiana Coalition Against Domestic Violence	P.O. Box 77308, Baton Rouge, LA 70809-7308	504-752-1296	504-751-8927
MAINE	Maine Coalition for Family Crisis Services	128 Main Street, Bangor, ME 04401	207-941-1194	207-941-2327
MARYLAND	Maryland Network Against Domestic Violence	6911 Laurel Bowie Road, Suite 309, Bowie, MD 20715	301-352-4574	301-809-0422
MASSACHU-SETTS	Massachusetts Coalition of Battered Women's Service Groups	14 Beacon Street, Suite 507, Boston, MA 02108	617-248-0922	617-248-0902
MICHIGAN	Michigan Coalition Against Domestic Violence and Sexual Assault	913 West Holmes, Suite 211, Lansing, MI 48910	517-887-9334	517-887-9348
MINNESOTA	Minnesota Coalition for Battered Women	450 North Syndicate Street, Suite 122, St. Paul, MN 55104	612-646-1109	612-646-1527

STATE	DEPARTMENT	ADDRESS	TELEPHONE	FAX
MISSOURI	Missouri Coalition Against Domestic Violence	415 East McCarty, Jefferson City, MO 65101	573-634-4161	573-636-3728
MISSISSIPPI	Mississippi State Coalition Against Domestic Violence	P.O. Box 4703, Jackson, MS 39296-4703	601-981-9196	601-981-2501
MONTANA	Montana Coalition Against Domestic Violence	P.O. Box 633, Helena, MT 59624	406-443-7794	406-443-7818
NEBRASKA	Nebraska Domestic Violence and Sexual Assault Coalition	315 South 9th - #18, Lincoln, NE 68508-2253	402-476-6256	n/a
NEVADA	Nevada Network Against Domestic Violence	2100 Capurro Way, Suite E, Sparks, NV 89431	702-358-1171	702-358-0546
NEW HAMPSHIRE	New Hampshire Coalition Against Domestic and Sexual Violence	P.O. Box 353, Concord, NH 03302-0353	603-224-8893	603-228-6096
NEW JERSEY	New Jersey Coalition for Battered Women	2620 Whitehorse/ Hamilton Square Road, Trenton, NJ 08690	609-584-8107	609-584-9750
NEW MEXICO	New Mexico State Coalition Against Domestic Violence	P.O. Box 25266, Albuquerque, NM 87125	505-246-9240	505-246-9434
NEW YORK	New York State Coalition Against Domestic Violence	79 Central Avenue, Albany, NY 12206	518-432-4864	518-463-3155
NORTH CAROLINA	North Carolina Coalition Against Domestic Violence	301 West Main Street, Suite 350, Durham, NC 27707	919-956-9124	919-682-1449
NORTH DAKOTA	North Dakota Council on Abused Women's Services	418 East Rosser Avenue, Suite 320, Bismarck, ND 58501	701-255-6240	701-255-1904
OHIO	Ohio Domestic Violence Network	4041 North High Street, Suite 400, Columbus, OH 4 3214-3247	614-784-0023	614-784-0033

STATE	DEPARTMENT	ADDRESS	TELEPHONE	FAX
OKLAHOMA	Oklahoma Coalition Against Domestic Violence and Sexual Assault	2200 N Classen Blvd., Suite 610, Oklahoma City, OK 73106	405-557-1210	405-557-1296
OREGON	Oregon Coalition Against Domestic and Sexual Violence	520 NW Davis, Suite 310, Portland, OR 97209	503-223-7411	503-223-7490
PENNSYL-VANIA	Pennsylvania Coalition Against Domestic Violence	6400 Flank Drive, Suite 1300, Harrisburg, PA 17112-2778	717-545-6400	717-671-8149
RHODE ISLAND	Rhode Island Coalition Against Domestic Violence	422 Post Road, Suite 104, Warwick, RI 02888	401-467-9940	401-467-9943
SOUTH CAROLINA	South Carolina Coalition Against Domestic Violence & Sexual Assault	P.O. Box 7776, Columbia, SC 29202-7776	803-750-1222	803-750-1246
SOUTH DAKOTA	South Dakota Coalition Against Domestic Violence and Sexual Assault	P.O. Box 141, Pierre, SD 57501	605-945-0869	605-945-0870
TENNESSEE	Tennessee Task Force Against Domestic Violence	P.O. Box 120972, Nashville, TN 37212	615-386-9406	615-383-2967
TEXAS	Texas Council on Family Violence	8701 North Mopac Expressway, Suite 450, Austin, TX 78759	512-794-1133	512-794-1199
UTAH	Utah Domestic Violence Advisory Council	120 North 200 West, Suite 425, Salt Lake City, UT 84103	801-538-4100	801-538-3993
VERMONT	Vermont Network Against Domestic Violence and Sexual Assault	P.O. Box 405, Montpelier, VT 05601	802-223-6943	802-223-6943
VIRGINIA	Virginians Against Domestic Violence	2850 Sandy Bay Road, Suite 101, Williamsburg, VA 23185	757-221-0990	757-229-1553

STATE	DEPARTMENT	ADDRESS	TELEPHONE	FAX
WASHINGTON	Washington State Coalition Against Domestic Violence	2101 4th Avenue E, Suite 103, Olympia, WA 98506	360-407-0756	360-352-4078
WEST VIRGINIA	West Virgina Coalition Against Domestic Violence	P.O. Box 85, 181B Main Street, Sutton, WV 26601-0085	304-965-3552	304-765-5071
WISCONSIN	Wisconsin Coalition Against Domestic Violence	1400 East Washington Avenue, Suite 232, Madison, WI 53703-0085	608-255-0539	608-255-3560
WYOMING	Wyoming Coalition Against Domestic Violence and Sexual Assault	P.O. Box 236, Laramie, WY 82073	307-755-5481	307-755-5482
NATIONAL	National Coalition Against Domestic Violence	P.O. Box 18749, Denver, CO 80218	303-839-1852	303-831-9251
NATIONAL	National Coalition Against Domestic Violence Policy Office	119 Constitution Avenue NE, Washington, D.C. 20002	202-544-7358	202-544-7893

APPENDIX 11:
DIRECTORY OF REGIONAL DOMESTIC
VIOLENCE ORGANIZATIONS

NAME	ADDRESS	TELEPHONE	FAX
Interagency Council Domestic Violence Program	1940 Mesquite Avenue, Lake Havasu City, AZ 86403	520-453-5800	520-453-2787
Southern California Coalition on Battered Women	6308 Woodman Avenue, Suite 117, Van Nuys, CA 91401	818-787-0072	818-787-0073
Delaware Domestic Violence Coordinating Council	900 King Street, Wilmington, DE 19801	302-577-2684	n/a
Georgia Coalition on Family Violence Inc.	1827 Powers Ferry Rd., Bldg 3, Suite 325, Atlanta, GA 30339	770-984-0085	770-984-0068
Victim's Services Domestic Violence Program	P.O. Box 15, McComb, IL 61455	309-837-6622	309-836-3640
Otter Tail County Intervention Project	Box 815, Fergus Falls, MN 56538	218-739-0983	n/a
Missouri Shores Domestic Violence Center	P.O. Box 398, Pierre, SD 57501	605-224-7187	605-244-0256
North Carolina Victim Assistance Network	505 Oberlin Road, Suite 151, Raleigh, NC 27605	919-831-2857	919-831-0824
Long Island Women's Coalition, Inc.	P.O. Box 1269M, Bay Shore, NY 11706-0537	516-666-8833	n/a
Action Ohio Coalition for Battered Women	20 South Front Street, Columbus, OH 43215	614-221-1255	614-221-6357
White Buffalo Calf Women's Shelter	P.O. Box 227, Mission, SD 57555	605-856-2317	605-856-2994
Women's Coalition of St. Croix	Box 2734, Christiansted St. Croix, VI 00822	809-773-9272	809-773-9062
Red Cliff Band of Lake Superior Chippewaw Family Violence Program	P.O. Box 529, Bayfield, WI 54814	715-779-3707	715-779-3711

APPENDIX 12:

RESOURCE DIRECTORY FOR WOMEN VICTIMS

NAME	ADDRESS	TELEPHONE NUMBER
ACTION	1100 Vermont Avenue N.W., Washington, DC 20525	202-934-9396
Black Indian Hispanic and Asian Women in Action	122 West Franklin Avenue, Suite 306, Minneapolis, MN 55404	612-870-1193
Center for the Prevention of Sexual and Domestic Violence	1914 North 34th Street, Suite 105, Seattle, WA 98103	800-562-6025
Center for Women Policy Studies	2000 P Street N.W., Suite 508, Washington, DC 20036	202-872-1770
EMERGE	280 Green Street, 2nd Floor, Cambridge, MA 02139	617-547-9870
National Center for Women and Family Law	799 Broadway, Room 402, New York, NY 10003	212-674-8200
National Coalition Against Sexual Assault	2428 Ontario Road N.W., Washington, DC 20009	202-483-7165
National Council on Jewish Women	53 West 23rd Street, New York, NY 10010	212-645-4048
National Organization for Women (NOW)	1000 16th Street N.W., Suite 700, Washington, DC 20036	202-331-0066
Women Against Abuse	P.O. Box 13758, Philadelphia, PA 19101	215-386-1280
Women's Legal Defense Fund	2000 P Street N.W., Suite 400, Washington, DC 20036	202-887-0364

APPENDIX 13:

JACOB WETTERLING
CRIMES AGAINST CHILDREN AND SEXUALLY
VIOLENT OFFENDER REGISTRATION ACT

TITLE XVII - CRIMES AGAINST CHILDREN

Subtitle A- Jacob Wetterling Crimes Against Children and Sexually Violent Offender Registration Act

SEC. 170101. ESTABLISHMENT OF PROGRAM

(a) In General-

(1) State guidelines- The Attorney General shall establish guidelines for State programs that require- (A) a person who is convicted of a criminal offense against a victim who is a minor or who is convicted of a sexually violent offense to register a current address with a designated State law enforcement agency for the time period specified in subparagraph (A) of subsection (b)(6); and

(B) a person who is a sexually violent predator to register a current address with a designated State law enforcement agency unless such requirement is terminated under subparagraph (B) of subsection (b)(6).

(2) Court determination- A determination that a person is a sexually violent predator and a determination that a person is no longer a sexually violent predator shall be made by the sentencing court after receiving a report by a State board composed of experts in the field of the behavior and treatment of sexual offenders.

(3) Definitions- For purposes of this section:

(A) The term "criminal offense against a victim who is a minor" means any criminal offense that consists of -

(i) kidnapping of a minor, except by a parent;

(ii) false imprisonment of a minor, except by a parent;

(iii) criminal sexual conduct toward a minor;

(iv) solicitation of a minor to engage in sexual conduct;

(v) use of a minor in a sexual performance;

(vi) solicitation of a minor to practice prostitution;

(vii) any conduct that by its nature is a sexual offense against a minor; or

(viii) an attempt to commit an offense described in any of clauses (i) through (vii), if the State-

(I) makes such an attempt a criminal offense; and

(II) chooses to include such an offense in those which are criminal offenses against a victim who is a minor for the purposes of this section. For purposes of this subparagraph conduct which is criminal only because of the age of the victim shall not be considered a criminal offense if the

(B) The term "sexually violent offense" means any criminal offense that consists of aggravated sexual abuse or sexual abuse (as described in sections 2241 and 2242 of title 18, United States Code, or as described in the State criminal code) or an offense that has as its elements engaging in physical contact with another person with intent to commit aggravated sexual abuse or sexual abuse (as described in such sections of title 18, United States Code, or as described in the State criminal code).

(C) The term "sexually violent predator" means a person who has been convicted of a sexually violent offense and who suffers from a mental abnormality or personality disorder that makes the person likely to engage in predatory sexually violent offenses.

(D) The term "mental abnormality" means a congenital or acquired condition of a person that affects the emotional or volitional capacity of the person in a manner that predisposes that person to the commission of criminal sexual acts to a degree that makes the person a menace to the health and safety of other persons.

(E) The term "predatory" means an act directed at a stranger, or a person with whom a relationship has been established or promoted for the primary purpose of victimization.

(b) Registration Requirement Upon Release, Parole, Supervised Release, or Probation-

An approved State registration program established under this section shall contain the following elements:

(1) Duty of state prison official or court -

(A) If a person who is required to register under this section is released from prison, or placed on parole, supervised release, or probation, a State prison officer, or in the case of probation, the court, shall-

(i) inform the person of the duty to register and obtain the information required for such registration;

(ii) inform the person that if the person changes residence address, the person shall give the new address to a designated State law enforcement agency in writing within 10 days;

(iii) inform the person that if the person changes residence to another State, the person shall register the new address with the law enforcement agency with whom the person last registered, and the person is also required to register with a designated law enforcement agency in the new State not later than 10 days after establishing residence in the new State, if the new State has a registration requirement;

(iv) obtain fingerprints and a photograph of the person if these have not already been obtained in connection with the offense that triggers registration; and

(v) require the person to read and sign a form stating that the duty of the person to register under this section has been explained.

(B) In addition to the requirements of subparagraph (A), for a person required to register under subparagraph (B) of subsection (a)(1), the State prison officer or the court, as the case may be, shall obtain the name of the person, identifying factors, anticipated future residence, offense history, and documentation of any treatment received for the mental abnormality or personality disorder of the person.

(2) Transfer of information to state and the FBI-

The officer, or in the case of a person placed on probation, the court, shall, within 3 days after receipt of information described in paragraph (1), forward it to a designated State law enforcement agency. The State law enforcement agency shall immediately enter the information into the appropriate State law enforcement record system and notify the appropriate law enforcement agency having jurisdiction where the person expects to reside. The State law enforcement agency shall also immediately transmit the conviction data and fingerprints to the Federal Bureau of Investigation.

(3) Verification-

(A) For a person required to register under subparagraph (A) of subsection (a)(1), on each anniversary of the person's initial registration date during the period in which the person is required to register under this section the following applies:

(i) The designated State law enforcement agency shall mail a nonforwardable verification form to the last reported address of the person.

(ii) The person shall mail the verification form to the designated State law enforcement agency within 10 days after receipt of the form.

(iii) The verification form shall be signed by the person, and state that the person still resides at the address last reported to the designated State law enforcement agency.

(iv) If the person fails to mail the verification form to the designated State law enforcement agency within 10 days after receipt of the form, the person shall be in violation of this section unless the person proves that the person has not changed the residence address.

(B) The provisions of subparagraph (A) shall be applied to a person required to register under subparagraph (B) of subsection (a)(1), except that such person must verify the registration every 90 days after the date of the initial release or commencement of parole.

(4) Notification of local law enforcement agencies of changes in address-

A change of address by a person required to register under this section reported to the designated State law enforcement agency shall be immediately reported to the appropriate law enforcement agency having jurisdiction where the person is residing. The designated law enforcement agency shall, if the person changes residence to another State, notify the law enforcement agency with which the person must register in the new State, if the new State has a registration requirement.

(5) Registration for change of address to another state-

A person who has been convicted of an offense which requires registration under this section shall register the new address with a designated law enforcement agency in another State to which the person moves not later than 10 days after such person establishes residence in the new State, if the new State has a registration requirement.

(6) Length of registration-

(A) A person required to register under subparagraph (A) of subsection (a)(1) shall continue to comply with this section until 10 years have elapsed since the person was released from prison, placed on parole, supervised release, or probation.

(B) The requirement of a person to register under subparagraph (B) of subsection (a)(1) shall terminate upon a determination, made in accordance with paragraph (2) of subsection (a), that the person no longer suffers from a mental abnormality or personality disorder that would make the person likely to engage in a predatory sexually violent offense.

(c) Penalty-

A person required to register under a State program established pursuant to this section who knowingly fails to so register and keep such registration current shall be subject to criminal penalties in any State in which the person has so failed.

(d) Release of Information-

The information collected under a State registration program shall be treated as private data except that-

(1) such information may be disclosed to law enforcement agencies for law enforcement purposes;

(2) such information may be disclosed to government agencies conducting confidential background checks; and

(3) the designated State law enforcement agency and any local law enforcement agency authorized by the State agency may release relevant information that is necessary to protect the public concerning a specific person required to register under this section, except that the identity of a victim of an offense that requires registration under this section shall not be released.

(e) Immunity for Good Faith Conduct-

Law enforcement agencies, employees of law enforcement agencies, and State officials shall be immune from liability for good faith conduct under this section.

(f) Compliance-

(1) Compliance date-

Subject to paragraph (2), each State shall have not more than 3 years from the date of enactment of this Act in which to implement this section, except that the Attorney General may grant an additional 2 years to a State that is making good faith efforts to implement this section.

(2) Ineligibility for funds-

(A) A State that fails to implement the program as described in this section shall not receive 10 percent of the funds that would otherwise be allocated to the State under section 506 of the Omnibus Crime Control and Safe Streets Act of 1968 (42 U.S.C. 3765).

(B) Reallocation of funds-

Any funds that are not allocated for failure to comply with this section shall be reallocated to States that comply with this section.

APPENDIX 14:

MEGAN'S LAW

SECTION 1. SHORT TITLE.

This Act may be cited as "Megan's Law".

SECTION 2. RELEASE OF INFORMATION AND CLARIFICATION OF PUBLIC NATURE OF INFORMATION.

Section 170101(d) of the Violent Crime Control and Law Enforcement Act of 1994 (42 U.S.C. 14071(d)) is amended to read as follows:

"(d) Release of Information.—

"(1) The information collected under a State registration program may be disclosed for any purpose permitted under the laws of the State.

"(2) The designated State law enforcement agency and any local law enforcement agency authorized by the State agency shall release relevant information that is necessary to protect the public concerning a specific person required to register under this section, except that the identity of a victim of an offense that requires registration under this section shall not be released.".

GLOSSARY

GLOSSARY

Abduction - The criminal or tortious act of taking and carrying away by force.

Accusation - An indictment, presentment, information or any other form in which a charge of a crime or offense can be made against an individual.

Accusatory Instrument - The initial pleading which forms the procedural basis for a criminal charge, such as an indictment.

Accuse - To directly and formally institute legal proceedings against a person, charging that he or she has committed an offense.

Acquit - A verdict of "not guilty" which determines that the person is absolved of the charge and prevents a retrial pursuant to the doctrine of double jeopardy.

Acquittal - One who is acquitted receives an acquittal, which is a release without further prosecution.

Adjourn - To briefly postpone or delay a court proceeding.

Adjudication - The determination of a controversy and pronouncement of judgment.

Admissible Evidence - Evidence which may be received by a trial court to assist the trier of fact, either the judge or jury, in deciding a dispute.

Admission - In criminal law, the voluntary acknowledgment that certain facts are true.

American Bar Association (ABA) - A national organization of lawyers and law students.

American Civil Liberties Union (ACLU) - A nationwide organization dedicated to the enforcement and preservation of rights and civil liberties guaranteed by the federal and state constitutions.

Appearance - To come into court, personally or through an attorney, after being summoned.

Arraign - In a criminal proceeding, to accuse one of committing a wrong.

Arraignment - The initial step in the criminal process when the defendant is formally charged with the wrongful conduct.

Arrest - To deprive a person of his liberty by legal authority.

Battery - The unlawful application of force to the person of another.

Bench Warrant - An order of the court empowering the police or other legal authority to seize a person.

Bodily Injury - Generally refers to any act, except one done in self-defense, that results in physical injury or sexual abuse.

Burden of Proof - The duty of a party to substantiate an allegation or issue to convince the trier of fact as to the truth of their claim.

Capital Crime - A crime for which the death penalty may, but need not necessarily, be imposed.

Capital Punishment - The penalty of death.

Child Abuse - Any form of cruelty to a child's physical, moral or mental well-being.

Child Custody - The care, control and maintenance of a child which may be awarded by a court to one of the parents of the child.

Child Protective Agency - A state agency responsible for the investigation of child abuse and neglect reports.

Child Support - The legal obligation of parents to contribute to the economic maintenance of their children.

Child Welfare - A generic term which embraces the totality of measures necessary for a child's well being; physical, moral and mental.

Circumstantial Evidence - Indirect evidence by which a principal fact may be inferred.

Court - The branch of government responsible for the resolution of disputes arising under the laws of the government.

Cross-Examination - The questioning of a witness by someone other than the one who called the witness to the stand concerning matters about which the witness testified during direct examination.

Cruelty - The intentional and malicious infliction of physical or mental suffering on one's spouse.

Culpable - Referring to conduct, it is that which is deserving of moral blame.

District Attorney - An officer of a governmental body with the duty to prosecute those accused of crimes. process standards of fairness and justice.

Domestic Violence - Generally refers to felony or misdemeanor crimes of violence committed by a current or former spouse of the victim, by a person with whom the victim shares a child in common, by a person who is cohabitating with or has cohabitated with the victim as a spouse, or by a person similarly situated to a spouse.

Duress - Refers to the action of one person which compels another to do something he or she would not otherwise do.

Felony - A crime of a graver or more serious nature than those designated as misdemeanors.

Fine - A financial penalty imposed upon a defendant.

Hearing - A proceeding to determine an issue of fact based on the evidence presented.

Homicide - The killing of a human being by another human being.

Illegal - Against the law.

Imprisonment - The confinement of an individual, usually as punishment for a crime.

Injury - Any damage done to another's person, rights, reputation or property.

Jail - Place of confinement where a person in custody of the government awaits trial or serves a sentence after conviction.

Judge - The individual who presides over a court, and whose function it is to determine controversies.

Jury - A group of individuals summoned to decide the facts in issue in a lawsuit.

Jury Trial - A trial during which the evidence is presented to a jury so that they can determine the issues of fact, and render a verdict based upon the law as it applies to their findings of fact.

Law Enforcement - Generally refers to public agencies charged with policing functions, including any of their component bureaus.

Legal Aid - A national organization established to provide legal services to those who are unable to afford private representation.

Malice - A state of mind that accompanies the intentional commission of a wrongful act.

Manslaughter - The unlawful taking of another's life without malice aforethought.

Mens Rea - A guilty mind.

Misdemeanor - Criminal offenses which are less serious than felonies and carry lesser penalties.

National Domestic Violence Hotline - A national, toll-free telephone hotline operated for the purpose of providing information and assistance to victims of domestic violence.

Not Guilty - The plea of a defendant in a criminal action denying the offense with which he or she is charged.

Offense - Any misdemeanor or felony violation of the law for which a penalty is prescribed.

Parole - The conditional release from imprisonment whereby the convicted individual serves the remainder of his or her sentence outside of prison as long as he or she is in compliance with the terms and conditions of parole.

Penal Institution - A place of confinement for convicted criminals.

Prosecutor - The individual who prepares a criminal case against an individual accused of a crime.

Protection Order - Generally refers to any injunction issued for the purpose of preventing violent or threatening acts of domestic violence or harassment, including temporary and final orders issued by civil or criminal courts.

Public Defender - A lawyer hired by the government to represent an indigent person accused of a crime.

Rape - The unlawful sexual intercourse with a female person without her consent.

Restitution - The act of making an aggrieved party whole by compensating him or her for any loss or damage sustained.

Self-Defense - The right to protect oneself, one's family, and one's property from an aggressor.

Sentence - The punishment given a convicted criminal by the court.

Testify - The offering of a statement in a judicial proceeding, under oath and subject to the penalty of perjury.

Testimony - The sworn statement make by a witness in a judicial proceeding.

Verdict - The definitive answer given by the jury to the court concerning the matters of fact committed to the jury for their deliberation and determination.

Victim Services - Generally refers to organizations that assist domestic violence or sexual assault victims, such as rape crisis centers and battered women's shelters.

Warrant - An official order directing that a certain act be undertaken, such as an arrest.

BIBLIOGRAPHY

BIBLIOGRAPHY AND ADDITIONAL READING

Black's Law Dictionary, Fifth Edition. St. Paul, MN: West Publishing Company, 1979.

Communities Against Violence Network (CAVNET) (Date Visited: May 1998), http://www.cavnet.org.

Domestic Violence Hotline Resource List (Date Visited: May 1998), http://www.feminist.org/911/crisis.html.

Evaluation Guidebook: Projects Funded by S.T.O.P. Formula Grants under the Violence Against Women Act (Date Visited: May 1998), http://www.urban.org/crime/evalguide.html.

Justice Information Center (Date Visited: May 1998), http://www.ncjrs.org/

National Coalition Against Sexual Assault (Date Visited: May 1998), http://www.achiever.com/freehmpg/ncas/.

Office of Justice Programs (Date Visited: May 1998), http://www.ojp.usdog.gov/.

Rape, Abuse and Incest National Network (Date Visited: May 1998), http://www.rainn.org/.

The U.S. Department of Health and Human Services (Date Visited: May 1998), http://www.os.dhhs.gov/.

The U.S. Department of Justice (Date Visited: May 1998), http://www.usdoj.gov/.